ONE-POT
COOKING

ONE-POT COOKING

SUE CUTTS
&
MARY MORRIS

Sundial

First published in 1981 by
Octopus Books Ltd
59 Grosvenor Street, London W1

© 1981 Hennerwood Publications Limited

ISBN 0 906320 27 5

Printed in England by Severn Valley Press Limited

CONTENTS

INTRODUCTION   6

EVERYDAY CASSEROLES   10

SPECIAL OCCASIONS   46

MEALS-IN-A-POT   68

AROUND THE WORLD   82

VEGETABLES   96

PARTY CASSEROLES   112

PUDDINGS   126

TOPPINGS & ACCOMPANIMENTS   140

INDEX   142

NOTES

1. Recipes for pressure cookers are denoted by a **P** symbol and those for slow cookers by an **S** symbol. All other recipes are for ordinary casserole dishes.

2. All recipes serve 4 unless otherwise stated.

3. All eggs are sizes 3, 4, 5 (standard) unless otherwise stated.

4. All spoon measurements are level.

5. Metric and imperial measurements have been calculated separately. Use one set of measurements only as they are not exact equivalents.

6. Preparation times given are an average calculated during recipe testing.

7. Cooking times may vary slightly depending on the individual oven. Dishes should be placed in the centre of the oven unless otherwise specified.

8. Always preheat the oven or grill to the specified temperature.

9. All sugar is granulated unless otherwise stated.

10. Spoon measures can be bought in both imperial and metric sizes to give accurate measurement of small quantities.

ACKNOWLEDGEMENTS

Photography: Robert Golden
Photographic styling: Antonia Gaunt
Preparation of food for photography:
Jackie Burrow

The publishers would like to thank
the following shops for the loan of props
for photography:

The Cutlery Shop at Bournes; Oxford Street
London W1

The Conran Shop; 77-79 Fulham Rd London SW3
Divertimenti; 68 Marylebone Lane London W1

The publishers would also like to thank
The Prestige Group Limited and TI Housewares
for their loan of pressure cookers and slow cookers.

INTRODUCTION

Casseroling is one of the most traditional and best-loved cooking methods, in which the blending of flavours, textures and colours provides a great deal of pleasure and satisfaction to even the most inexperienced of cooks.

Among the many advantages that casseroling has over other cooking methods is the generally uncomplicated preparation: once the ingredients are cooking, the dish usually requires no more attention. Casseroled food can be kept hot without spoiling, which is a great help when entertaining, and can be successfully reheated without losing flavour. In fact, many casseroled dishes are improved in flavour and quality when reheated. Many of the dishes can also be brought straight from the oven to the table for serving.

What is a casserole? Quite simply, casseroling is cooking food in a small amount of liquid in a tightly closed ovenproof or flameproof dish, in the oven, or on top of the cooker. When roasting, frying or grilling, the outside of meat is very quickly cooked to seal in the juices; however, during the prolonged cooking process of casseroling, the juices seep out into the sauce and the meat gradually becomes tender. This is why the cheaper cuts of meat are so well suited to this method of cooking. If you are using beef for casseroling, the best buys are thin flank, leg, shin, chuck, blade, sticking, clod or skirt. With veal, breast, neck, shoulder or knuckle are recommended; if you are using lamb, then breast, scrag or neck, trimmed of excess fat, are the most suitable. The more expensive cuts of pork can be casseroled, but the cheaper cuts such as hand of pork and spare rib make very appetizing dishes. Even belly of pork can be used provided you do not mind fatty food.

Casseroles are ideal for storing in the freezer, to have on hand when you want a quick but substantial meal. When preparing a casserole for freezing you should use cornflour, or a mixture of cornflour and flour, rather than ordinary flour as the thickening agent because, during freezing, cornflour will not break down as ordinary flour does.

The dishes in which you can make a casserole come in all shapes, sizes and designs, and may be made from heat-resistant glass, enamelled iron, earthenware, stainless steel, aluminium, copper or porcelain. All the casserole dishes are ovenproof, but the most versatile ones are those which are also flameproof, because they can be used on top of the cooker as well as in the oven. Not all casserole dishes are flameproof, so remember to check the label when buying and using them.

The thicker the casserole dish the better, too. Although it may take longer to bring the contents inside a thick casserole to the boil (unless the casserole is metal), there is less likelihood of the food sticking and burning during the long cooking process.

There may be times when you will need a shallow casserole dish, especially for meat or fish with a topping such as a lattice of pastry, or piped potatoes. Generally, however, the deeper the casserole dish the better, to ensure even cooking. Those which were traditionally used for making Lancashire Hot Pot were especially tall and straightsided, so that the long-boned chops from the Pennine sheep could line the sides, before the kidneys, oysters and everything else were packed in the centre. Now, with the smaller English and New Zealand lamb, almost any deep casserole dish will do for Hot Pot.

It is worth remembering that no matter how delicious a casserole might taste, without proper presentation, toppings and garnish, it will still look just like any other stew. You will find that some interesting recipes for toppings, such as seasoned crumbs, cheese straw pastry, sausage meat balls and herb and nut dumplings have been included. These give a casserole eye appeal and they are all easy to make.

SLOW ELECTRIC COOKERS

While casseroling is one of the most convenient of cooking methods, it does not always fit in with the hectic life style which most of us lead today. For a busy cook, an electric slow cooker is a boon. These cookers allow long, slow cooking, completely unattended; the only real difference between them and traditional casseroles is that they are powered by electricity instead of the open fire or range.

Electric slow cookers can be used to make all kinds of stews, ragoûts and braises, and the long period of cooking in moist conditions tenderizes even the toughest meats. Slow cookers are also suitable for cooking pâtés, soups, fish dishes and desserts, or even heating wine for hot punch at a party.

All electric slow cookers on the market today have a similar basic design. Each comprises a metal or plastic case into which the stoneware or earthenware cooking pot is fitted. The pot itself may be fixed into the case, or have a lift-out facility. The heating element is located either around the sides, or under the base, of the pot. This location is entirely dependent on the size and design of the cooker. The element is not thermostatically controlled and does not need to be. The power going into the slow cooker is very low, as little as 55 watts on small models, and it is this low wattage which allows the cooker and, therefore, the food to heat and cook slowly over many hours.

For greater versatility and convenience the majority of slow cookers have two heat settings. The low setting allows the longest cooking times, so that the food can cook all day. This can be anything from 7 to 12 or even 14 hours depending on the recipe. The high setting generally reduces the times on low by about half. Therefore a recipe normally taking 8 hours on low, will cook in about 4 hours on high. For those cookers which only have one setting this will be equivalent to the low cook on 2-heat cookers.

An added benefit to the user of an electric slow cooker is that, in general, cooking times are fairly flexible. This is more apparent on the low setting where many recipes can be left cooking for several hours longer than required without spoiling. There are, however, exceptions to this rule, namely rice or pasta dishes, and guidance for the best results with these foods are given in the manufacturer's handbook.

Due to the low heat input and consequent gradual heat build up, some models of electric slow cookers have special instructions for the commencement of cooking. For example, you may be told to preheat the empty slow cooker for 20 minutes before adding the food, or the recipe may recommend a preliminary short cooking period on the high setting before turning to low. Some slow cookers overcome the inconvenience of this latter point by having an 'auto' setting. This means that the cooker switches itself from high to low.

The overall design of the slow cooker, and its capacity, will, of course, dictate the scope of recipes you can cook. Those slow cookers with 'lift-out' stoneware pots allow many recipes to be finished with a topping in the oven or, if they are shallow enough, to be browned under a grill. These pots are also usually wider in design, so they can accommodate larger joints of meat or whole fish. The taller, narrower design of pot usually means slight adaptations to the recipe and food preparation. For example, fish may need boning and rolling and ingredients may need to be layered. Again these points are covered in each manufacturer's handbook.

One or two slow cookers on the market have a flameproof lift-out cooking pot in which meat or poultry can be browned before the slow cooking begins. The majority of slow cookers, however, do not have flameproof pots, and the prebrowning has to be done in a frying pan.

Once cooking commences, the slow cooker is left unattended. Stirring is only necessary for rice dishes to assist in the even absorption of the liquid. Taking the lid off frequently during cooking will cause a substantial heat loss and increase the cooking time.

All the electric slow cooker recipes in this book have been tested with a number of different makes of slow cooker. However, because there are slight variations in their recommended use, i.e. preheating and two-heat cooking, it is very important to refer to and follow the basic rules given by each manufacturer's handbook.

PRESSURE COOKERS

What can a pressure cooker offer that an ordinary hotplate, oven or electric slow cooker cannot? Answer, speed of cooking. Where traditional casseroling relies on long slow cooking for best results, the pressure cooker is designed to save time and fuel while still keeping all the versatility the other methods offer.

A pressure cooker is basically a saucepan with a cover, which is sealed. By sealing the two parts together the steam, which normally escapes into the atmosphere, is held in and the consequent build-up of pressure which the trapped steam causes is controlled by a pressure 'weight' or valve. This steam tenderizes the less expensive cuts of meat and poultry, just as traditional slow casseroling does – but much more quickly.

All pressure cookers are completely safe to use and many have their safety endorsed by the British Standards Institute whose Kite Mark is stamped on the cooker base. It is certainly worth looking for one of these models.

The pressure cookers available today have come a long way in their design and ease of use, compared with those cookers available even 5 years ago. New features are the inclusion of a clockwork timer on one model, which is linked with an automatic release of pressure when the cooking time is complete. All you have to do is to turn off the heat when the bell rings. On other cookers there is a manual release of pressure when the cooking is completed, so that you no longer have to move the cooker to a sink of cold water to

reduce the pressure. A trivet and other accessories allow you to cook several foods at the same time.

All pressure cookers cook quickly, but some are available with only lower pressure weights or valves. This simply means that these cookers will need slightly longer cooking times. The standard pressure weights are marked H. (6.75 kg/15 lb), M (4.5 kg/10 lb) or L (2.25 kg/5 lb). The H pressure is the pressure most used. However, some foods, or recipes, are better suited to lower pressures; this is indicated in the recipe itself.

The recipes in this book are written to use the standard H, M or L pressures. If you own a cooker that has only a 'LOW' pressure facility it is important to refer to your handbook to obtain the correct cooking times. However, as a general rule, if a recipe indicates the use of H pressure, allow one and a half times the cooking time when cooking with a 'LOW' pressure cooker.

The methods for closing the cooker, bringing to pressure and release of pressure vary slightly from cooker to cooker, so follow the instructions recommended by the manufacturer.

However, there are five golden rules to follow when using a pressure cooker and these apply to all pressure cookers:
1. *Always read and follow the manufacturer's instructions.*
2. *Remember to add the liquid*; the minimum quantity is generally 300 ml/ ½ pint. As a general rule the liquid should be the first item to be added to the cooker, unless you are using the cooker base to pre-brown ingredients.
3. *The cooker must not be over-filled.* When cooking liquid foods such as soups or casseroles the cooker 'base' should not be more than half full. When cooking solid foods such as a selection of vegetables the 'whole' cooker should not be more than two-thirds full (the 'whole' cooker is the height of the base and cover together).
4. *Time foods carefully.* For foods that only require very short cooking times this is very important as even an extra minute will result in overcooked and unacceptable results.
5. *Reduce pressure completely before attempting to remove the weight or opening the cooker.* There are two basic methods to do this.
   (a) Quickly – carry the cooker to the sink and place it in cold water; if the cooker has its own pressure release mechanism this is operated while the cooker is still on the stove.
   (b) Slowly – remove from the heat and leave to stand at room temperature for 10-15 minutes.

All containers used in the pressure cooker must be boilable, if they are plastic, and completely ovenproof if they are glass or ceramic. Neither of these types of container should be used with a fixed lid; cover with foil or greaseproof paper.

All the pressure cooker recipes in this book have been tested with a number of different makes of family size pressure cookers and are written to serve 4 people. If you own a pressure cooker which is small, adjustments to the recipes may be necessary to avoid overfilling.

EVERYDAY CASSEROLES

RUSSIAN CABBAGE

Preparation time: 1 hour
Cooking time: about 2 hours
Oven: 150°C, 300°F, Gas Mark 2

1 medium cabbage, trimmed
2 tablespoons oil
1 onion, peeled and finely
  chopped
50 g/2 oz button mushrooms,
  sliced
1 tablespoon chopped fresh
  parsley
1 teaspoon chopped fresh
  thyme
75 g/3 oz long-grain rice
450 g/1 lb lean minced beef
salt
freshly ground black pepper
1 × 750 g/1½ lb can tomatoes,
  sliced with their juice
juice of 1 large lemon
1 teaspoon sugar
TO GARNISH:
garlic-flavoured croûtons
1 tablespoon chopped fresh
  parsley

1. Put the cabbage head down into a large heatproof bowl and pour over boiling water to cover. Leave for 30 minutes, then drain well.

2. Separate the leaves and cut out the thick centre rib. When you reach the centre and can no longer separate the leaves, cut away and discard the core, then chop the remaining cabbage finely.

3. Heat 1 tablespoon of the oil in a large frying pan, add the onion and fry gently until softened. Stir in the mushrooms, parsley, thyme, rice and beef, and season with salt and pepper. Toss well over a brisk heat until the meat begins to colour.

4. Remove from the heat and leave to cool slightly then stir in the chopped cabbage.

5. Place a little of this stuffing in the centre of each cabbage leaf, fold in the edges and roll into parcels. Pour the remaining oil into a casserole and pack the cabbage rolls, seam side down, into the dish.

6. Add the tomatoes, the lemon juice and sprinkle the sugar over the cabbage rolls. Season lightly with salt and pepper, then cover and cook in a preheated oven for about 2 hours.

7. Halfway through the cooking time, check the liquid level; the cabbage leaves must not dry out, so if necessary add a little beef stock. Serve garnished with croûtons, and chopped parsley.

AMERICAN BEEF & CHEESE

Preparation time: 20 minutes
Cooking time: 1 hour
Oven: 150°C, 300°F, Gas Mark 2

2 tablespoons oil
450 g/1 lb minced beef
1 medium onion,
  peeled and finely chopped
1 stick celery, finely chopped
1 × 275 g/10 oz can condensed
  tomato soup
salt
freshly ground black pepper
75 g/3 oz cottage cheese
75 g/3 oz full fat soft cheese
2 tablespoons soured cream
100 g/4 oz ribbon noodles,
  cooked and drained

1. Heat the oil in a large frying pan, add the beef, onion and celery and cook over a brisk heat to brown the meat.
2. Drain off the surplus fat, then stir in the undiluted soup. Season lightly with salt and pepper and bring very gently to the boil.
3. Remove from the heat and mix in the cottage and cream cheeses, soured cream and the noodles. Check the seasoning.
4. Pour the mixture into a casserole, cover and bake in a preheated oven for 1 hour.
5. Purée of parsnips and a green vegetable are good accompaniments to this dish.

BEEF WITH GUINNESS

Preparation time: 15 minutes
Cooking time: 1½ hours
Oven: 150°C, 300°F, Gas Mark 2

100 g/4 oz unsmoked bacon,
  rind removed, diced
750 g/1½ lb chuck steak,
  trimmed and cut into 2½
  cm/1 inch cubes
salt
freshly ground black pepper
2 tablespoons oil
1 medium onion,
  peeled and finely chopped
150 ml/¼ pint beef stock
300 ml/½ pint Guinness
1 teaspoon dark brown sugar
40 g/1½ oz sultanas
2 tablespoons Cheese Croûtons
  (page 141), to garnish

1. Toss the bacon and chuck steak in flour seasoned with salt and pepper.
2. Heat the oil in a large frying pan, add the meat and onion and fry over a brisk heat until the meat is browned. Transfer the meat to a casserole.
3. Sprinkle any remaining seasoned flour into the pan and cook gently for 2 minutes, stirring well. Stir in the stock, Guinness, brown sugar and sultanas. Bring to the boil and add salt and pepper to taste. Pour into the casserole, cover and cook in a preheated oven for 1½ hours. Serve sprinkled with Cheese Croûtons.

BEEF & HORSERADISH CASSEROLE

P

Preparation time: 10 minutes
Cooking time: H pressure 25 minutes

2 tablespoons oil
1 medium onion,
  peeled and chopped
100 g/4 oz button mushrooms
750 g/1½ lb shin of beef, cut
  into 2.5 cm/1 inch cubes
1 tablespoon creamed
  horseradish
½ teaspoon dry mustard
600 ml/1 pint beef stock
salt
TO FINISH:
150 ml/¼ pint soured cream
1 tablespoon chopped chives

1. Heat the oil in the open cooker. Add the onion and fry until lightly browned. Add the mushrooms and continue frying for 1-2 minutes. Lift out the vegetables, draining well, and set aside.
2. Add the meat cubes to the cooker and brown on all sides. Remove the cooker from the heat and return the vegetables to it. Stir in the horseradish, mustard, stock and a little salt.
3. Close the cooker, bring to H pressure and cook for 25 minutes. Reduce the pressure quickly.
4. Stir in the soured cream and taste and adjust the seasoning. Sprinkle with the chives before serving.

RICH BEEF & KIDNEY CASSEROLE S

Preparation time: 15 minutes
Cooking time: Low 8-10 hours
*   High 4-5 hours*

1 tablespoon oil
450 g/1 lb stewing beef,
    trimmed of excess fat and cut
    into 2.5 cm/1 inch cubes
225 g/8 oz pig's kidney,
    skinned, cored and cut into
    1 cm/½ inch pieces
1 medium onion,
    peeled and chopped
1 × 400 g/14 oz can tomatoes,
    chopped, with their juice
50 g/2 oz mushrooms,
    thickly sliced
pinch of dried mixed herbs
150 ml/¼ pint beef stock
salt
freshly ground black pepper
2 teaspoons cornflour
1 tablespoon cold water

1. Heat the oil in a frying pan. Add the beef cubes and brown on all sides. Add the kidney and continue cooking for 1 minute. Transfer the meat to the stoneware pot, draining well.
2. Add the onion to the frying pan and fry until lightly browned. Stir in the tomatoes, mushrooms, herbs, stock and salt and pepper to taste. Bring to the boil, then pour over the meat in the stoneware pot.
3. Cover and cook on Low for 8-10 hours or High for 4-5 hours.
4. Thirty minutes before the cooking time is finished, dissolve the cornflour in the cold water and stir into the mixture in the pot until the liquid has thickened. Taste and adjust the seasoning.
5. Serve the plain boiled potatoes and a green vegetable.

BEEF JAVA

Preparation time: 15 minutes
Cooking time: 2-2½ hours
Oven: 150°C, 300°F, Gas Mark 2

2 onions, peeled and sliced
750 g-1 kg/1½-2 lb stewing
    steak, cut into 2.5 cm/1 inch
    cubes
600 ml/1 pint beef stock
1 garlic clove,
    peeled and crushed
6 parsley stalks
salt
freshly ground black pepper
50 g/2 oz long-grain rice
50 g/2 oz seedless raisins
50 g/2 oz blanched almonds,
    sliced
1 tablespoon paprika
finely chopped fresh parsley,
    to garnish

Thick flank (from the belly) or shin (from the foreleg) are particularly suitable cuts for this stew. Both give well-flavoured gravy.

1. Melt the dripping in a large frying pan, add the onions and cook gently until golden brown. Remove and put into a casserole.
2. Add the meat to the frying pan and cook over a brisk heat for 3-4 minutes to brown. Drain and mix with the onions in the casserole. Add the stock, garlic, parsley stalks, and salt and pepper to taste. Cover and cook in a preheated oven for 1¾-2 hours.
3. Stir in the rice, raisins, almonds and paprika. Re-cover and continue cooking for 30-45 minutes or until the meat and rice are tender.
4. Serve sprinkled with chopped parsley, and accompanied by mango chutney.

Top left: American beef and cheese
Top right: Rich beef and kidney casserole
Centre left: Beef with Guinness
Centre right: Beef Java
Bottom: Beef and horseradish casserole

BRAISED BEEF WITH ORANGE

Preparation time: 15 minutes
Cooking time: 2 hours
Oven: 150°C, 300°F, Gas Mark 2

2 tablespoons oil
450 g/1 lb braising steak,
    trimmed and cut into 2½
    cm/1 inch cubes
1 large onion,
    peeled and thinly sliced
1 garlic clove,
    peeled and crushed
75 g/3 oz long-grain rice
300 ml/½ pint beef stock
finely grated rind and juice of
    2 oranges
salt
freshly ground black pepper
50 g/2 oz pimiento-stuffed
    green olives, rinsed and
    drained
TO GARNISH:
1 orange, peeled and thinly
    sliced
1 tablespoon chopped fresh
    parsley

1. Heat the oil in a large pan, add the steak and onion and fry gently until lightly coloured. Stir in the garlic and rice and cook for 2 minutes. Add the stock and grated orange rind, mix well and season with salt and pepper. Bring to the boil, then transfer to a casserole.
2. Cover and cook in a preheated oven for 1½ hours.
3. Stir in the olives and orange juice and return the casserole, uncovered, to the oven for a further 30 minutes.
4. Adjust the seasoning, then serve garnished with twisted orange slices sprinkled with parsley.

Right: Braised beef with orange
Far right: Beef and pepper casserole

BEEF DUBONNET

Serves: 8
Preparation time: 30 minutes
Cooking time: 1¼ hours
Oven: 160°C, 325°F, Gas Mark 3

1 kg/2 lb rump steak,
    cut into thin strips
50 g/2 oz seasoned flour
4 tablespoons oil
3 onions, peeled and thinly sliced
2 bay leaves
2 cloves
300 ml/½ pint Dubonnet
150 ml/¼ pint beef stock
salt
freshly ground black pepper
300 ml/½ pint soured cream
2 tablespoons chopped fresh
    parsley
TO GARNISH:
mashed potato nests
cooked peas

1. Toss the steak strips in the seasoned flour.
2. Heat the oil in a large frying pan, add the steak and brown it. Transfer to a casserole.
3. Add the onions to the pan and cook gently until soft and golden. Add any remaining seasoned flour, mix well and cook for 2 minutes.
4. Stir in the bay leaves, cloves, Dubonnet and stock and bring slowly to the boil. Season to taste with salt and pepper, then pour the sauce over the steak.
5. Cover the casserole and cook in a preheated oven for 1 hour or until the steak is tender.
6. Stir in the soured cream and parsley and adjust the seasoning. Return the casserole to the oven to heat through. Remove the cloves and bay leaves.
7. Pour into a heated serving dish and surround with the potato nests filled with peas.

Right: Beef Dubonnet

BEEF & PEPPER CASSEROLE

Preparation time: 25 minutes
Cooking time: 1½ hours
Oven: 150℃, 300°F, Gas Mark 2

225 g/8 oz unsmoked streaky
   bacon, rind removed, diced
2 onions, peeled and sliced
750 g/1½ lb braising steak,
   trimmed and cut into 6 cm/
   2½ inch cubes
2 carrots, scraped and sliced
2 garlic cloves,
   peeled and crushed
450 ml/¾ pint beef stock
2 teaspoons wine vinegar
2 teaspoons caraway seeds
2 large green peppers,
   cored, seeded and sliced
salt
freshly ground black pepper
2 teaspoons cornflour
TOPPING:
1 tablespoon walnut halves,
   lightly toasted
1 tablespoon chopped fresh
   parsley

1. Fry the bacon in a dry flameproof casserole over a gentle heat until the fat runs. Add the onions, meat and carrots and toss over a brisk heat until the meat is browned.
2. Stir in the garlic, stock, wine vinegar, caraway seeds, green peppers and salt and pepper to taste. Bring to the boil, then cover and cook in a preheated oven for 1½ hours.
3. Remove the casserole from the oven. Dissolve the cornflour in a little of the gravy and stir back into the stew. Bring to the boil on top of the stove, stirring until thickened.
4. Sprinkle the walnuts and parsley on top and serve.

LANCASHIRE HOT POT

Preparation time: 25 minutes
Cooking time: 2-2½ hours
Oven: 170°C, 325°F, Gas Mark 3

50 g/2 oz plain flour
salt
freshly ground black pepper
2 tablespoons dripping
750 g/1½ lb best end neck of
    lamb, trimmed and cut into
    cutlets
4 lambs' kidneys,
    skinned, cored and halved
3 onions, peeled and sliced
3 carrots, scraped and sliced
4 medium potatoes,
    peeled and quartered
450 ml/¾ pint chicken stock
sprig of fresh thyme, or pinch
    of dried thyme
1 teaspoon anchovy essence
    (optional)
2 tablespoons chopped fresh
    parsley, to garnish

The tall, straight-sided hot pot was specially designed for the large, long-boned sheep from the Pennines, but now that New Zealand and small English lamb is widely available any casserole dish can be used. Oysters (being cheap at that time) were traditional in the true Lancashire hot pot; the anchovy essence gives an idea of the flavour.

1. Season the flour with salt and pepper. Melt the dripping in a large frying pan. Dip each cutlet in the seasoned flour, then place in the pan and brown on both sides.
2. If you have the tall pot, stand the cutlets in it, heads down, and place the kidneys between them. Otherwise lay the cutlets and kidneys in any deep casserole.
3. Add the onions and carrots to the frying pan and cook gently until softened. Lift out and put into the casserole. Arrange the potatoes over the top.
4. Sprinkle the remaining seasoned flour into the frying pan and cook for 2 minutes, then stir in the stock. Bring to the boil. Add the thyme and anchovy essence and check the seasoning.
5. Pour the mixture over the potatoes. Cover the casserole and cook in a preheated oven for 1½ hours.
6. Remove the lid, baste the potatoes with a little of the gravy and season lightly with salt and pepper. Continue cooking until the potatoes are tender and brown. Serve sprinkled with the parsley.

WINTER LAMB CASSEROLE   P

Preparation time: 10 minutes
Cooking time: H pressure 15 minutes

2 tablespoons cooking oil
1 medium onion,
    peeled and sliced
1 medium parsnip, peeled and
    cut into 2.5 cm/1 inch cubes
1 medium turnip, peeled and
    cut into 2.5 cm/1 inch cubes
2 medium carrots,
    scraped and thickly sliced
8 thin best end of neck lamb
    chops
1 tablespoon tomato purée
450 ml/¾ pint beef stock
¼ teaspoon dried mixed herbs
salt
freshly ground black pepper

1. Heat the oil in the open cooker. Add the onion, parsnip, turnip and carrots and fry gently for 2-3 minutes. Lift out the vegetables, draining well, and set aside.
2. Add the chops to the cooker and brown on both sides. Lift out the chops.
3. Put all the vegetables back into the cooker and lay the chops on top. Mix together the tomato purée, stock, herbs and salt and pepper to taste and pour over the chops.
4. Close the cooker, bring to H pressure and cook for 15 minutes. Reduce the pressure quickly.
5. Taste and adjust the seasoning, then serve the chops surrounded by the vegetables.

Above left: Lancashire hot pot
Above right: Breast of lamb ragoût

Right: Winter lamb casserole

BREAST OF LAMB RAGOÛT S

Preparation time: 30 minutes
Cooking time: Low 8-10 hours
*   High 4-5 hours*

2 tablespoons oil
1 medium onion,
    peeled and chopped
225 g/8 oz carrots,
    scraped and sliced
1 medium parsnip, peeled and
    cut into 1 cm/½ inch cubes
2 breasts of lamb, well trimmed
    of fat and cut into single rib
    pieces
1 × 225 g/8 oz can tomatoes,
    chopped, with their juice
150 ml/¼ pint beef stock
½ teaspoon dried rosemary
salt
freshly ground black pepper
2 teaspoons cornflour
1 tablespoon cold water

1. Heat the oil in a frying pan. Add the onion, carrots and parsnip and fry until they are lightly browned. Transfer to the stoneware pot, draining well.
2. Add the lamb pieces to the frying pan and brown on all sides. Transfer to the stoneware pot.
3. Add the tomatoes, stock, rosemary and salt and pepper to taste to the frying pan and bring to the boil, stirring well. Pour over the meat and vegetables in the stoneware pot.
4. Cover and cook on Low for 8-10 hours or High for 3-4 hours.
5. Lift out some of the lamb pieces. Dissolve the cornflour in the cold water and stir into the sauce until it has thickened. Return the lamb and continue cooking for a few minutes to reheat it. Taste and adjust the seasoning before serving.

SPICY LAMB

S

Preparation time: 10 minutes
Cooking time: Low 8-10 hours
  High 4-5 hours

2 tablespoons cooking oil
1 large onion,
  peeled and chopped
8 good sized best end of neck
  lamb chops, trimmed of
  excess fat
finely grated rind of 1 orange
2 tablespoons orange juice
2 tablespoons tomato purée
1 tablespoon demerara sugar
1 teaspoon dry mustard
¼ teaspoon ground ginger
300 ml/½ pint hot beef stock
salt
1 tablespoon cornflour
1½ tablespoons cold water
orange slices, to garnish

1. Heat the oil in a frying pan. Add the onion and cook until lightly browned. Transfer to the stoneware pot, draining well.
2. Add the chops to the pan and brown on both sides. Transfer to the stoneware pot.
3. Mix together the orange rind and juice, tomato purée, sugar, mustard, ginger and stock. Pour over the chops and season lightly with salt.
4. Cover and cook on Low for 8-10 hours or High for 4-5 hours.
5. Lift out four of the chops. Dissolve the cornflour in the cold water and stir into the sauce until it has thickened. Return the chops and continue cooking for a few minutes to reheat them. Taste and adjust the seasoning.
6. Garnish with slices of orange to serve.

CASSOULET

Preparation time: 1½ hours, plus
  soaking time
Cooking time: 3½ hours
Oven: 170°C 325°F, Gas Mark 3

225 g/½ lb dried white haricot
  beans, soaked in water
  overnight
750 ml/1¼ pints beef stock
100 g/4 oz fresh pork rind,
  diced
8 garlic cloves, peeled
1 carrot,
  trimmed and lightly scraped
3 onions, peeled
4 cloves
2 tablespoons oil
100 g/4 oz lean pork, cubed
100 g/4 oz salt pork, cubed
350 g/12 oz boned lamb
  shoulder, cubed
1 × 425 g/15 oz can tomatoes
  with their juice
bouquet garni
salt
freshly ground black pepper
350 g/12 oz garlic sausage or
  boiling ring, cut into 5
  cm/2 inch lengths
50 g/2 oz fresh breadcrumbs
2 tablespoons chopped fresh
  parsley, to garnish

The true French cassoulet calls for preserved goose and a rather involved method of cooking; this is a simplified adaptation.

1. Drain the soaked beans and put them into a large saucepan with the stock, pork rind, 4 whole garlic cloves, the carrot and 1 onion stuck with the cloves. Cover, bring slowly to the boil and simmer for 1 hour.
2. Strain off the liquid and reserve. Discard the carrot, onion and garlic. Put the beans and pork rind into a deep casserole.
3. Heat the oil in a large frying pan, add the pork, salt pork and lamb and brown on all sides. Lift out and add to the beans in the casserole.
4. Thinly slice the remaining onions and fry gently in the fat until softened. Stir in the tomatoes, the remaining garlic, crushed, the bean cooking liquid, the bouquet garni and salt and pepper to taste.
5. Bring to the boil and pour over the beans. Mix all the ingredients well together, then cover the casserole and cook in a preheated oven for 2½ hours.
6. Remove the lid and carefully stir in the sausage pieces. Adjust the seasoning. Sprinkle the crumbs evenly over the top and return to the oven, uncovered. Cook for a further hour. The fat will rise to the surface to turn the crumbs into a crisp golden topping.

Above left: Spicy lamb
Above right: Peppered pork
Above centre: Cassoulet

7. Do not allow the cassoulet to get too dry during the cooking; add a little more stock if necessary. The final dish should have a creamy consistency. Garnish with parsley before serving.

PEPPERED PORK

S

Preparation time: 8 minutes
Cooking time: Low 7-9 hours
  High 3-4 hours

1 tablespoon oil
1 small onion, peeled and sliced
1 red or green onion pepper, cored, seeded and sliced
4 pork sparerib chops, trimmed of excess fat
1 teaspoon paprika
1 tablespoon tomato purée
300 ml/½ pint chicken stock
salt
2 teaspoons cornflour
1 tablespoon cold water

1. Heat the oil in a frying pan. Add the onion and red or green pepper and fry gently until the onion begins to colour. Transfer the vegetables to the stoneware pot, draining well.
2. Add the chops to the frying pan and brown well on both sides. Transfer to the stoneware pot, laying them on top of the vegetables.
3. Stir the paprika and tomato purée into the sediment in the frying pan, then add the stock and a little salt. Bring to the boil, stirring, and pour over the chops.
4. Cover and cook on Low for 7-9 hours or High for 3-4 hours.

5. Lift out the chops. Set aside and keep hot. Dissolve the cornflour in the cold water and stir into the sauce until it has thickened. Taste and adjust the seasoning. Return the chops to the sauce and reheat for a few moments before serving.

PORK & TOMATO POT ROAST

P

Preparation time: 10 minutes
Cooking time: H pressure 45 minutes

2 tablespoons oil
1½ kg/3 lb blade bone of pork,
    well trimmed of fat
salt
freshly ground black pepper
1 large onion,
    peeled and chopped
1 × 400 g/14 oz can tomatoes,
    chopped, with their juice
1 teaspoon dried marjoram
300 ml/½ pint beef stock
1 teaspoon cornflour
2 teaspoons cold water

1. Heat the oil in the open cooker. Season the joint well with salt and pepper. Place it in the cooker and brown on all sides. Lift out the joint and set aside.
2. Add the onion to the cooker and fry gently until it is transparent.
3. Remove the cooker from the heat and stir in the tomatoes, marjoram and stock. Return the joint to the cooker.
4. Close the cooker, bring to H pressure and cook for 45 minutes. Reduce the pressure quickly.
5. Lift out the joint. Slice it thickly and arrange on a heated serving dish. Keep hot.

6. Return the open cooker to the heat. Mash the vegetables into the cooking liquid in the cooker. Dissolve the cornflour in the cold water and add to the vegetable mixture. Bring to the boil and simmer, stirring, for 1-2 minutes or until the sauce has thickened. Taste and adjust the seasoning.
7. Pour the sauce over the meat and serve immediately.

SPARE RIBS WITH BEANS

Preparation time: 1½ hours, plus
    soaking time
Cooking time: about 3½ hours
Oven: 150°C, 300°F, Gas Mark 2

175 g/6 oz dried haricot beans,
    soaked in water overnight
1 kg/2 lb pork spareribs,
    cut into pieces
3 tablespoons soy sauce
1 chicken stock cube
1 onion,
    peeled and finely chopped
1 tablespoon soft brown sugar
2 tablespoons molasses
1 teaspoon dry mustard
1 teaspoon Worcestershire
    sauce
salt
freshly ground black pepper
spring onion brushes,
    to garnish

1. Drain the soaked beans, put them into a saucepan, cover with plenty of fresh cold water, bring to the boil, cover and simmer for 1 hour.
2. Meanwhile, arrange the spareribs on the rack in the grill pan, lightly brush them with the soy sauce and grill until brown on both sides.
3. Drain the beans, reserving 600 ml/1 pint of the cooking liquid, and dissolve the stock cube in it.
4. Mix together the beans, onion, brown sugar, molasses, mustard, Worcestershire sauce and a little salt and pepper.
5. Layer the spareribs and the bean mixture in a casserole, finishing with spare ribs. Pour in enough of the stock mixture barely to cover. Cover and cook in a preheated oven for 2 hours.
6. Uncover and continue cooking for 1-1½ hours or until the beans are tender and the rib topping is crisp.
7. The liquid will reduce as the beans absorb it; do not allow the dish to get dry, so add a little more stock if necessary.
8. Serve garnished with spring onion brushes.

Top: Pork and tomato pot roast
Right: Spare ribs with beans
Far right: Pork and tomato with kasha

PORK & TOMATO WITH KASHA

Preparation time: 25 minutes
Cooking time: 1½ hours
Oven: 160°C, 325°F, Gas Mark 3

750 g/1½ lb pork shoulder
50 g/2 oz butter
2 onions,
   peeled and finely chopped
75 g/3 oz kasha
   (buckwheat groats)
1 teaspoon ground cumin
6 tomatoes, skinned and sliced
600 ml/1 pint veal or chicken
   stock
salt
freshly ground black pepper
sprigs of parsley, to garnish

Kasha is available from wholefood and health food shops and some large supermarkets.

1. Remove the rind from the pork and cut it into very thin strips. Cut the pork into 5 cm/2 inch pieces.
2. Melt the butter in a frying pan, add the pork rind strips and fry carefully, until crisp. Drain on kitchen paper and reserve.
3. Add the pork pieces to the pan and brown lightly on all sides, then transfer to a casserole. Add the onions to the pan and cook gently until soft and golden.
4. Stir in the kasha, cumin, tomatoes, stock and salt and pepper to taste. Bring to the boil and pour over the meat in the casserole.
5. Cover and cook in a preheated oven for 1½ hours or until the pork is tender.
6. After 1 hour check the casserole is not drying out – the kasha absorbs liquid as it swells, so add a little more stock if necessary. However, the resultant dish should not be 'wet'.
7. Arrange the reserved pork rind strips over the dish with the parsley sprigs and serve with a green vegetable in season or a salad.

PORK RASHERS WITH PLUMS

Preparation time: 25 minutes
Cooking time: 1½ hours
Oven: 180°C, 350°F, Gas Mark 4

450 g/1 lb red plums,
    halved and stoned
2 tablespoons soft brown sugar
2 tablespoons oil
8 pork rashers, about 2 cm/
    ¾ inch thick, rind removed
1 onion, peeled and thinly sliced
2 garlic cloves,
    peeled and crushed
1 teaspoon chopped fresh sage or
    ½ teaspoon dried sage
3 tablespoons chicken stock
3 tablespoons dry cider or white
    wine
salt
freshly ground black pepper
TO GARNISH:
lemon twists
sprigs of parsley

Pork rashers, sometimes called streaky pork is cut from pork belly.

1. Put the plums on the bottom of a casserole and sprinkle with the brown sugar.
2. Heat the oil in a frying pan, add the pork and brown on each side. Remove from the pan and reserve. Add the onion to the pan and cook gently until softened. Stir in the garlic and sage.
3. Add the onion mixture to the plums. Pour in the stock and cider or wine and season to taste with salt and pepper. Mix well together, then arrange the pork over the top.
4. Cover and cook in a preheated oven for 1 hour.
5. Remove the lid, baste the pork with the plum juice and return to the oven. Cook for a further 30 minutes or until the pork is tender, golden and glazed. Adjust the seasoning. Garnish with lemon and parsley and serve.

PORK CHOPS BRAMLEY-STYLE

Preparation time: 30 minutes
Cooking time: 1¾-2 hours
Oven: 180°C, 350°F, Gas Mark 4

2 teaspoons oil
4 pork chops, ¾ inch thick,
    rind removed
salt
freshly ground black pepper
3 medium Bramley apples,
    peeled, cored and sliced
150 ml/¼ pint chicken stock
150 ml/¼ pint apple juice
4 fresh sage leaves, chopped, or
    ½ teaspoon dried sage
2 medium potatoes,
    peeled and sliced
4 streaky bacon rashers,
    rind removed, diced
1 onion, peeled and chopped
TO GARNISH:
1 tablespoon toasted chopped
    walnuts
2 teaspoons chopped fresh
    parsley

In this recipe, the apples will 'fall', making a sauce, and the potatoes will absorb and thicken the liquid. Choose floury potatoes.

1. Heat the oil in a frying pan, add the chops and brown on both sides. Transfer to a casserole. Season the meat with salt and pepper. Cover with half the apple slices.
2. Mix together the stock, apple juice and sage and pour a little over the apple. Cover with half the potatoes, season with salt and pepper, add a little more of the liquid, then the remaining apples, liquid and potatoes.
3. Put the bacon into the frying pan and cook gently until the fat runs. Add the onion and cook until golden. Spread the brown mixture over the potatoes.
4. Cover and cook in a preheated oven for 1 hour 35 minutes. Remove the lid and continue cooking until the potatoes are tender.
5. Garnish with the walnuts and parsley, and serve with broccoli, dressed with butter and lemon juice.

IRISH HOT POT

Preparation time: 20 minutes
Cooking time: 1¾-2¼ hours
Oven: 170°C, 325°F, Gas Mark 3

750 g/1½ lb unsmoked slipper
   joint of bacon, rind removed,
   trimmed and cut into 2.5
   cm/1 inch cubes
3 medium onions,
   peeled and thinly sliced
5 carrots, scraped and sliced
2 sticks celery, sliced
salt
freshly ground black pepper
750 g/1½ lb small potatoes,
   peeled, or large potatoes
   thickly sliced
light ham-flavoured or
   vegetable stock, to cover
15 g/½ oz butter, melted
2 tablespoons chopped fresh
   parsley, to garnish

1. Put the bacon cubes in a saucepan and cover with cold water. Bring slowly to the boil, then drain well.
2. Mix together the onions, carrots and celery, and season lightly with salt and pepper. Put a layer of the potatoes into deep casserole, cover with a layer of bacon cubes and then with the mixed vegetables. Continue making layers, ending with potatoes.
3. Pour in the stock; it should barely cover the ingredients. Cover the casserole and cook in a preheated oven for 1½ hours.
4. Uncover and brush the potatoes on top with the melted butter. Continue cooking, uncovered, until the stock has reduced and the potatoes are tender. Serve sprinkled with parsley.
5. Equal quantities of finely chopped pickled beetroot and horseradish sauce beaten together makes an unusual and delicious accompaniment.

BACON & BUTTER BEAN CASSEROLE [P]

Preparation time: 10 minutes,
   plus soaking time
Cooking time: H pressure 15 minutes

100 g/4 oz dried butter beans
2 tablespoons oil
750 g/1½ lb unsmoked collar or
   forehock bacon joint, boned
   and cut into 2.5 cm/1 inch
   cubes
1 medium onion,
   peeled and sliced
2 sticks celery, chopped
600 ml/1 pint chicken stock or
   water
2 teaspoons chopped fresh
   parsley
freshly ground black pepper
2 teaspoons cornflour
1 tablespoon cold water

1. Put the beans into a bowl. Cover with boiling water and leave to soak for 1 hour. Drain the beans.
2. Heat the oil in the open cooker. Add the bacon, onion and celery and brown lightly.
3. Remove the cooker from the heat and stir in the stock or water, 1 teaspoon of the parsley, the drained beans and a little pepper.
4. Close the cooker and bring to H pressure. Cook for 15 minutes. Reduce the pressure quickly.
5. Dissolve the cornflour in the cold water. Stir into the mixture in the cooker and return the open cooker to the heat. Bring to the boil, stirring, for 1-2 minutes or until the sauce has thickened. Taste and adjust the seasoning.
6. Serve sprinkled with the remaining parsley.

Top: Pork rashers with plums
Above right: Irish hot pot
Above left: Pork chops Bramley-style
Bottom: Bacon and butter bean casserole

HAWAIIAN HAM

Preparation time: 15 minutes
Cooking time: 30 minutes
Oven: 180℃, 350°F, Gas Mark 4

4 gammon steaks, rind removed
50 g/2 oz butter
2 teaspoons soft brown sugar
25 g/1 oz plain flour
1 × 425 g/15 oz can crushed
   pineapple
50 g/2 oz seedless raisins
2 teaspoons Dijon mustard
salt
freshly ground black pepper
3 tablespoons double cream
25 g/1 oz toasted flaked
   almonds, to garnish

1. Snip the gammon fat to prevent it curling.
2. Melt the butter in a frying pan, add the gammon steaks, sprinkle them with the sugar and brown lightly on each side. Transfer the gammon to a casserole.
3. Sprinkle the flour into the frying pan and cook gently for 3-4 minutes. Stir in the crushed pineapple, raisins and mustard. Season with plenty of pepper, and, if necessary, a little salt (the gammon may be salty enough).
4. Bring to the boil, stirring, and cook for 2-3 minutes. Pour the sauce over the gammon, cover the casserole and cook in a preheated oven for 30 minutes.
5. Remove the lid, trickle the cream over the top and garnish with the flaked almonds.
6. Serve with baked jacket potatoes, and a green salad tossed with garlic French dressing.

THEATRE SUPPER

Preparation time: 20 minutes
Cooking time: 30 minutes
Oven: 180℃, 350°F, Gas Mark 4

225 g/8 oz vermicelli,
   cooked and drained
2 onions, peeled and grated
225 g/8 oz cooked ham or bacon,
   diced
2 tablespoons chopped fresh
   parsley
salt
freshly ground black pepper
50 g/2 oz butter
50 g/2 oz plain flour
600 ml/1 pint creamy milk
50 g/2 oz Parmesan cheese,
   grated
2 teaspoons caraway seeds
thin green and red pepper rings,
   to garnish

1. Mix together the vermicelli, onion, ham or bacon and parsley. Season with a little salt and plenty of pepper.
2. Melt the butter in a flameproof casserole, stir in the flour and cook gently for 3-4 minutes. Gradually pour in the milk, stirring, and bring to the boil. Simmer for 5 minutes.
3. Stir in the cheese and caraway seeds with salt and pepper to taste. Carefully fold in the vermicelli mixture. Cover the casserole and cook in a preheated oven for 30 minutes.
4. Garnish with the pepper rings and serve with an orange, watercress and almond salad.

FRANKFURTERS VICHY

Preparation time: 30 minutes
Cooking time: 1½-1¾ hours
Oven: 170°C, 325°F, Gas Mark 3

50 g/2 oz butter
2 onions,
    peeled and thinly sliced
1 stick celery, thinly sliced
6 carrots,
    lightly scraped and sliced
2 garlic cloves,
    peeled and crushed
40 g/1½ oz plain flour
200 ml/⅓ pint dry white wine
200 ml/⅓ pint chicken stock
1 tablespoon tomato purée
pinch of sugar
salt
freshly ground black pepper
8 frankfurters, cut into 5
    cm/2 inch lengths
4 potatoes, peeled and cut into
    2½ cm/1 inch cubes
SEASONED BUTTER:
100 g/4 oz butter or margarine,
    softened
1 garlic clove, peeled and
    crushed
2 tablespoons finely chopped
    fresh parsley
1 tablespoon lemon juice

1. Melt the butter in a flameproof casserole, add the onions, celery and carrots and cook gently until softened.
2. Stir in the garlic and flour and cook for 2-3 minutes. Stir in the wine, stock, purée, sugar and salt and pepper to taste. Bring to the boil, stirring, for 5 minutes.
3. Mix in the frankfurters and cover the top with the potato cubes.
4. To make the seasoned butter, beat all the ingredients together and add salt and pepper to taste.
5. Brush the potato cubes with half of the seasoned butter. Cover and cook in a preheated oven for 1½ hours.
6. Remove the lid, brush the potatoes with the remaining seasoned butter and continue cooking until the potatoes are tender and golden. Garnish with celery leaves and serve with hot sauerkraut.

HAM & CABBAGE CASSEROLE

Preparation time: 15 minutes
Cooking time: 45 minutes
Oven: 180°C, 350°F, Gas Mark 4

50 g/2 oz butter
50 g/2 oz plain flour
450 ml/¾ pint milk
1 teaspoon caraway seed or
    grated nutmeg
450 g/1 lb boiled ham or bacon,
    cut into 2.5 cm/1 inch cubes
1 small tight white cabbage,
    trimmed and finely shredded
salt
freshly ground black pepper
TO GARNISH:
1 onion, peeled and sliced into
    rings
a little milk
plain flour, seasoned
oil for deep frying

1. Melt the butter in a large saucepan. Stir in the flour and cook for 3-4 minutes. Gradually stir in the milk over a low heat and then bring to the boil. Add the caraway seed or nutmeg, the ham or bacon and cabbage. Season with salt and pepper and turn into a casserole.
2. Cover and cook in a preheated oven for 45 minutes or until the ham or bacon is tender.
3. Meanwhile, soak the onion rings in the milk for a few minutes, then shake off the excess. Use the flour to coat the onion, then deep fry the onion rings until crisp and golden brown. Drain on kitchen paper. Garnish the casserole with onion rings.
4. Sauté potatoes and whole baked tomatoes are ideal with this simple, wholesome dish.

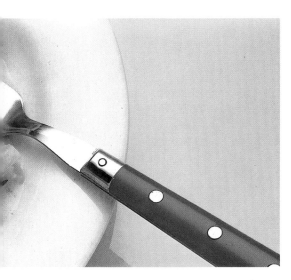

Top: Hawaiian ham
Above left: Theatre supper
Above right: Frankfurters vichy

Left: Ham and cabbage casserole

COUNTRY CASSEROLE

Preparation time: 1 hour
Cooking time: 1 hour
Oven: 150°C, 300°F, Gas Mark 2
* 200°C, 400°F, Gas Mark 6*

450 g/1 lb pork sausage meat
1-2 tablespoons seasoned flour
2 tablespoons oil

ONION SAUCE:
25 g/1 oz butter
2 onions,
  peeled and finely chopped
25 g/1 oz plain flour
300 ml/½ pint milk, or chicken
  stock and milk
salt
freshly ground black pepper
750 g/1¾ lb creamed potato,
  seasoned
2 oz strong Cheddar cheese,
  grated
sprig of fresh sage, to garnish

1. Divide the sausage meat into 8 pieces. Shape each one into a cake, and lightly coat with the seasoned flour.
2. Heat the oil in a large frying pan, and cook the patties gently on each side until lightly coloured. Drain and arrange in a deep casserole.
3. To make the onion sauce, melt the butter in a small saucepan, add the onions and cook very gently until soft but not coloured. Stir in the flour and cook for 2 minutes.
4. Gradually add the milk, stirring constantly, then bring to the boil and simmer for 10 minutes. Season to taste with salt and pepper. Pour the onion sauce over the meat, cover and cook in a preheated oven for 45 minutes.

5. Remove the casserole from the oven, uncover and pipe or spoon the creamed potato over the top, right to the edge. Sprinkle with the cheese.
6. Raise the oven temperature and replace the casserole, uncovered, for about 20 minutes, or until golden brown. Garnish with sage.

Below left: Bacon and sausage special
Centre: Country casserole
Below right: Savoury bacon and onion roll

BACON & SAUSAGE SPECIAL

Preparation time: 25 minutes
Cooking time: 55 minutes
Oven: 170°C, 325°F, Gas Mark 3

100 g/4 oz long grain rice
salt
2 teaspoons oil
450 g/1 lb pork or turkey
  sausage
50 g/2 oz butter
2 onions,
  peeled and finely chopped
300 ml/½ pint canned or bottled
  tomato juice
2 sprigs fresh basil,
  finely chopped, or 1 bay leaf
freshly ground black pepper
4 tomatoes,
  skinned and thickly sliced
8 thin streaky bacon rashers,
  rind removed
sprigs of parsley, to garnish

1. Add the rice to a saucepan of rapidly boiling salted water, then cover and cook for 10 minutes or until barely tender.
2. Meanwhile, heat the oil in a frying pan, add the sausages and brown on all sides.
3. Melt the butter in a flameproof casserole, add the onions and cook gently until softened. Add the drained rice and turn it over to absorb the butter. Stir in the tomato juice, basil or bay leaf and salt and pepper to taste.
4. Bury the sausages in the rice mixture. Top with the tomato slices and season with salt and pepper. Cover and cook in a preheated oven for 40 minutes.
5. Remove the lid and make a lattice with the streaky bacon over the top. Cook for a further 15 minutes or until the topping is crisp.
6. Garnish with parsley sprigs and serve with buttered cabbage.

SAVOURY BACON & ONION ROLL

P

Preparation time. 20 minutes
Cooking time: Steaming 10 minutes
L pressure 35 minutes

225 g/8 oz self-raising flour
½ teaspoon salt
100 g/4 oz shredded suet
1 teaspoon dried mixed herbs
150 ml/¼ pint cold water
900 ml/1½ pints boiling water
little lemon juice or vinegar
FILLING:
225 g/8 oz smoked back bacon,
 rind removed, chopped
1 medium onion,
 peeled and grated
50 g/2 oz mushrooms, chopped
salt
freshly ground black pepper

1. Sift the flour and salt into a mixing bowl. Stir in the suet and herbs with enough of the cold water to form a smooth elastic dough which leaves the sides of the bowl clean.
2. Turn the dough on to a floured surface and knead lightly. Roll out the dough to an oblong a little narrower than the bottom of the cooker and about 5 mm/ ¼ inch thick.
3. For the filling, mix together the bacon, onion and mushrooms with a little salt and pepper. Spread the mixture evenly over the dough oblong, taking it almost to the edges.
4. Brush the edges of the dough with a little water and roll up like a Swiss roll, sealing all the edges well.

5. Place the roll, seam side down, on a double thickness of greased greaseproof paper or on a well-greased piece of foil. Wrap loosely, making a pleat in the centre to allow for expansion. (Secure greaseproof paper with string at the ends; the foil can be pinched together.)
6. Place the trivet in the cooker, rim side down, and pour in the boiling water and lemon juice or vinegar. Bring back to the boil, then carefully place the pudding on the trivet.
7. Close the cooker and steam for 10 minutes (without the weights). Raise the heat, bring to L pressure and cook for 35 minutes. Reduce the pressure slowly.
8. Serve the pudding sliced, with a brown gravy and green vegetables.

OSSO BUCCO

Preparation time: 30 minutes
Cooking time: about 2 hours

25 g/1 oz butter
2 tablespoons olive oil
1 kg/2 lb shin of veal,
    sawn into 5 cm/2 inch pieces
1 onion, peeled and thinly sliced
450 g/1 lb tomatoes,
    skinned and sliced, or
    1 × 750 g/1 lb 10 oz can
    tomatoes with their juice
1 garlic clove,
    peeled and crushed
150 ml/¾ pint dry white wine
150 ml/¼ pint veal or chicken
    stock
1 bay leaf
salt
freshly ground black pepper
GREMOLATA:
2 tablespoons chopped fresh
    parsley
1 garlic clove,
    peeled and finely chopped
grated rind of 1 small lemon

1. Melt the butter with the oil in a flameproof casserole, add the veal and brown on all sides. Transfer the veal to a warm plate
2. Add the onion to the pot and cook gently until soft and golden.
3. Stir in the tomatoes, with their juice if using canned tomatoes, the garlic and white wine. Allow to bubble for a few minutes, then return the meat to the casserole, with the stock and bay leaf. Season with salt and pepper.
4. Cover and simmer gently for 2 hours or until the meat is really tender and the sauce is rich and thick.
5. Meanwhile, mix together the parsley, garlic and lemon rind.
6. Serve the veal sprinkled with the gremolata, accompanied by risotto milanese (rice cooked with white wine, saffron and beef marrow).

Right: Osso bucco

OXTAIL CARBONNADE　S

Preparation time: 15 minutes
Cooking time: Low 10-12 hours
　　　　High 5-6 hours

1 tablespoon oil
1 kg/2 lb oxtail, trimmed of
　　excess fat and chopped
1 large onion, peeled and sliced
2 medium carrots,
　　scraped and sliced
300 ml/½ pint brown ale
1 bouquet garni
salt
freshly ground black pepper
2 teaspoons cornflour
1 tablespoon cold water
chopped fresh parsley, to
　　garnish

1.　Heat the oil in a frying pan. Add the oxtail pieces and brown on all sides. Transfer them to the stoneware pot, draining well.
2.　Add the onion and carrots to the frying pan and fry until the onion is lightly browned. Transfer the vegetables to the stoneware pot. Drain off the fat left in the frying pan.
3.　Put the brown ale in the frying pan and bring to the boil, stirring in the sediment in the pan. Pour over the ingredients in the stoneware pot. Add the bouquet garni and salt and pepper to taste.
4.　Cover and cook on Low for 10-12 hours or High for 5-6 hours.
5.　Thirty minutes before the cooking time is finished, discard the bouquet garni. Dissolve the cornflour in the cold water and stir into the sauce until it has thickened.
6.　Before serving, taste and adjust the seasoning. Serve sprinkled liberally with chopped parsley.

OXTAIL CASSEROLE

Preparation time: 20 minutes
Cooking time: 2½-3 hours
Oven: 160°C, 325°F, Gas Mark 3

2 tablespoons oil
2 oxtails,
　　cut into 5 cm/2 inch sections
2 medium onions,
　　peeled and thinly sliced
2 sticks celery, thinly sliced
½ teaspoon chilli powder
2 teaspoons Dijon mustard
300 ml/½ pint plus 2
　　tablespoons fresh, frozen or
　　canned orange juice
2 tablespoons lemon juice
450 ml/¾ pint beef stock
salt
freshly ground black pepper
2 teaspoons cornflour
100 g/4 oz button mushrooms,
　　quartered
blanched strips of orange rind,
　　to garnish

This casserole is best made a day in advance in order to make removing the fat an easy job.

1.　Heat the oil in a large frying pan, add the oxtail pieces and brown on all sides. Transfer to a flameproof casserole.
2.　Add the onions and celery to the frying pan and cook gently until softened.
3.　Stir in the chilli powder, mustard, 300 ml/½ pint of the orange juice, the lemon juice, beef stock and salt and pepper to taste. Bring to the boil, then pour it over the oxtails in the casserole.
4.　Cover and cook in a preheated oven for 2 hours or until the meat is very tender.
5.　Lift the oxtails into a warm dish and remove the meat from the bones. Keep hot.
6.　Skim the fat from the sauce. Mix the cornflour with the remaining orange juice and add to the casserole with the mushrooms.
7.　Place the casserole over the heat on top of the stove and bring to the boil, stirring. Simmer for 1 minute.
8.　Return the meat to the casserole and reheat gently. Do not allow to boil.
9.　Garnish with the strips of orange rind and serve with creamed potato and a green vegetable.

Far left: Oxtail carbonnade
Left: Oxtail casserole

RABBIT & TARRAGON FRICASSEE   P

Preparation time: 12 minutes
Cooking time: H pressure 20
* minutes*

1 tablespoon oil
1 rabbit, jointed
1 medium onion,
  peeled and sliced
100 g/4 oz mushrooms, sliced
1 teaspoon dried tarragon
1 bay leaf
450 ml/¾ pint chicken stock
salt
freshly ground black pepper
TO FINISH:
1 egg yolk
2 tablespoons single cream or
  top of the milk

1. Heat the oil in the open cooker. Add the rabbit pieces and brown on all sides. Lift them out, draining well, and set aside.
2. Add the onion and mushrooms to the cooker and fry gently until the onion is just beginning to colour.
3. Return the rabbit pieces to the cooker and add the tarragon, bay leaf, stock and salt and pepper to taste. Stir well.
4. Close the cooker, bring to H pressure and cook for 20 minutes. Reduce the pressure quickly.
5. Lift out the rabbit pieces and place them on a heated serving dish. Discard the bay leaf.

6. Return the open cooker to the heat and thoroughly reheat the cooking liquid. Remove from the heat. Mix the egg yolk with the cream or top of milk and stir into the liquid. Continue stirring for a few minutes until the sauce thickens. Taste and adjust the seasoning, then pour the sauce over the rabbit.

Below left: Rabbit and tarragon fricassee
Centre: Hasenpfeffer
Below right: Rabbit and leeks

HASENPFEFFER

Preparation time: 20 minutes,
* plus 24 hours marinating time*
Cooking time: 1 hour 5 minutes
Oven: 150°C, 300°F, Gas Mark 2

1 kg/2 lb rabbit joints
150 ml/¼ pint water
3 tablespoons wine vinegar
200 ml/⅓ pint red wine
1 onion, peeled and sliced
2 bay leaves
4 cloves
salt
freshly ground black pepper
50 g/2 oz plain flour
3 tablespoons oil
2 teaspoons soft brown sugar
150 ml/¼ pint soured cream
2 tablespoons diced green
pepper, to garnish

This is a rich rabbit stew from Germany.

1. Put the rabbit into a large bowl with the water, vinegar, red wine, onion, bay leaves, cloves and salt and pepper. Cover and leave to marinate in the refrigerator for 24 hours, turning the joints once or twice.
2. Drain the rabbit, reserving the marinade and dry the joints with kitchen paper. Mix the flour with the salt and pepper and use to coat the rabbit joints.
3. Heat the oil in a flameproof casserole, add the rabbit joints and fry gently until lightly coloured on all sides. Remove from the heat.
4. Strain the marinade over the rabbit and stir carefully to incorporate any flour on the bottom of the pot. Bring to the boil, then cover and cook in a preheated oven for 1 hour.
5. Stir in the brown sugar and soured cream, check the seasoning and reheat gently on top of the stove.
6. Garnish with the green pepper. Serve with buttered ribbon noodles.

RABBIT & LEEKS

Preparation time: 15 minutes
Cooking time: 1¼ hours
Oven: 150 ℃, 300°F, Gas Mark 2

50 g/2 oz seasoned flour
1 × 1 kg/2 lb rabbit, jointed
3 tablespoons oil
4 leeks, white part only, sliced
450 ml/¾ pint chicken stock
1 bay leaf
sprig of fresh thyme, or
   pinch of dried thyme
salt
freshly ground black pepper
150 ml/¼ pint double cream
2 teaspoons Dijon mustard, or
   more to taste
few thin red pepper rings,
   to garnish

1. Use the seasoned flour to coat the rabbit joints.
2. Heat the oil in a flameproof casserole, add the rabbit joints and brown lightly. Lift on to a heated dish.
3. Add the leeks to the pot and cook gently for 5 minutes. Sprinkle in any remaining seasoned flour, mix well and cook for 2 minutes.
4. Stir in the stock, bay leaf and thyme and season lightly with salt and pepper. Bring to the boil, then return the rabbit to the casserole.
5. Cover and cook in a preheated oven for 1 hour or until the rabbit is tender.
6. Lift the joints on to a heated dish and keep hot.
7. Bring the sauce to the boil on top of the stove and boil until reduced by

one-third. Discard the bay leaf and thyme sprig.
8. Mix the cream and mustard together and stir into the sauce. Adjust the seasoning. Replace the rabbit in the casserole and heat gently; do not allow to boil.
9. Garnish with red pepper rings, and serve with potato croquettes and buttered carrots.

CONTINENTAL LIVER CASSEROLE P

Preparation time: 15 minutes
Cooking time: H pressure 6 minutes

2 tablespoons oil
1 medium onion,
    peeled and chopped
1 garlic clove,
    peeled and crushed
25 g/1 oz plain flour
salt
freshly ground black pepper
750 g/1½ lb pig's liver,
    cut into 1 cm/½ inch slices
1 × 400 g/14 oz can tomatoes,
    chopped, with their juice
300 ml/½ pint brown stock
1 teaspoon dried basil
1 × 100 g/4 oz packet frozen
    whole French beans, thawed
    and cut into 2.5 cm/1 inch
    pieces

1. Heat the oil in the open cooker. Add the onion and garlic and fry until the onion is transparent. Lift them out, draining well, and set aside.
2. Season the flour with salt and pepper and use to coat the liver. Add the liver to the cooker and brown on all sides.
3. Remove the cooker from the heat. Return the onions and garlic to the cooker with the tomatoes, stock, basil and beans. Add a little more salt and pepper and stir well.
4. Close the cooker, bring to H pressure and cook for 6 minutes. Reduce the pressure quickly.
7. Taste and adjust the seasoning, then serve with noodles.

SCANDINAVIAN LIVER

Preparation time: 30 minutes
Cooking time: 1 hour
Oven: 160°C, 325°F, Gas Mark 3

50 g/2 oz butter
2 medium onions,
    peeled and finely chopped
2 dessert apples,
    peeled, cored and finely diced
75 g/3 oz long-grain rice,
    cooked for 10 minutes and
    drained
300 ml/½ pint hot beef stock
1 egg, beaten
pinch of ground cloves
2 tablespoons soured cream
350 g/12 oz lamb's liver, minced
salt
freshly ground black pepper
TO GARNISH:
6 streaky bacon rashers,
    rind removed
chopped fresh parsley

1. Melt the butter in a frying pan, add the onions and fry until softened. Add the apples and cook for 5 minutes.
2. Turn into a mixing bowl and add the rice, stock (hot but not boiling), beaten egg, cloves, soured cream and liver. Toss gently together with a fork and season to taste with salt and pepper.
3. Pour into a lightly greased casserole. Cover and cook in a preheated oven for 45 minutes.
4. Remove the lid and continue cooking uncovered for 15 minutes.
5. Meanwhile, grill or fry the bacon rashers until crisp. Drain on kitchen paper, then crumble and mix with plenty of chopped parsley.
6. Serve the liver sprinkled with the bacon and parsley topping.

Top left: Continental liver casserole
Top right: Lamb's liver with coriander
Bottom left: Scandinavian liver
Bottom right: Kidney and sausage braise

LAMB'S LIVER WITH CORIANDER

Preparation time: 20 minutes,
   plus soaking time
Cooking time: 1 hour
Oven: 160°C, 325°F, Gas Mark 3

450 g/1 lb lamb's liver,
   cut into thin slices
50 g/2 oz seasoned flour
1 teaspoon dry mustard
salt
freshly ground black pepper
3 tablespoons oil
2 medium onions,
   peeled and finely chopped
2 medium cooking apples,
   peeled, cored and diced
300 ml/½ pint stock
1 teaspoon ground coriander
8 prunes, soaked and stoned
8 thin streaky bacon rashers,
   rind removed
chopped fresh parsley,
   to garnish

1. Dry the liver with kitchen paper.
2. Mix the seasoned flour with the mustard and use to coat each slice of liver. Heat the oil in a flameproof casserole, add the liver slices and brown lightly on each side. Lift on to a plate.
3. Add the onions to the pot and cook gently until softened, then add the apples and cook for a further 2 minutes. Sprinkle in any remaining seasoned flour and cook, stirring, for 2 minutes.
4. Stir in the stock and coriander, and bring to the boil. Season to taste with salt and pepper.
5. Replace the liver in the casserole, cover and cook in a preheated oven for 40 minutes.
6. Meanwhile, wrap each drained prune in a rasher of bacon. Remove the casserole lid, place the bacon rolls on top of the liver and return to the oven, uncovered. Continue cooking for 20 minutes or until the bacon rolls are cooked.
7. Garnish with chopped parsley, and serve with creamed potato and green beans.

KIDNEY & SAUSAGE BRAISE

Preparation time: 20 minutes
Cooking time: 45 minutes
Oven: 160°C, 325°F, Gas Mark 3

50 g/2 oz seasoned flour
salt
freshly ground black pepper
450 g/1 lb beef kidney,
   skinned, cored and sliced
225 g/8 oz pork chipolatas
2 tablespoons oil
1 onion,
   peeled and finely chopped
2 carrots, scraped and sliced
300 ml/½ pint beef stock
100 g/4 oz mushrooms, sliced
squeeze of lemon juice
1 bouquet garni
2 tablespoons redcurrant jelly
Rosemary Croûtons (page 141),
   to garnish

1. Use the seasoned flour to coat the kidney and sausages.
2. Heat the oil in a frying pan, add the kidney and sausages and brown them lightly. Transfer the kidneys and sausages to a casserole.
3. Add the onion and carrots to the frying pan and cook gently for 5 minutes. Sprinkle in any remaining seasoned flour, mix well and cook for 2 minutes.
4. Stir in the stock and bring to the boil. Add the mushrooms, lemon juice and bouquet garni and season to taste with salt and pepper.
5. Pour into the casserole, then cover and cook in a preheated oven for 35 minutes.
6. Stir in the redcurrant jelly, re-cover and cook for a further 10 minutes. Adjust the seasoning. Discard the bouquet garni.
7. Garnish with croûtons before serving.

PAPRIKA LIVER CASSEROLE [S]

Preparation time: 10 minutes
Cooking time: Low 6-8 hours
*   High 3-4 hours*

750 g/1½ lb pig's liver, sliced
25 g/1 oz plain flour
salt
freshly ground black pepper
2 tablespoons cooking oil
1 medium onion,
    peeled and thinly sliced
2 teaspoons paprika
300 ml/½ pint beef stock
1 × 225 g/8 oz can red
    pimento, drained and sliced
½ teaspoon caraway seeds

1. Wash the liver and dry thoroughly. Mix the flour with salt and pepper and use to coat the liver, shaking off the excess.
2. Heat the oil in a frying pan. Add the liver and onion and fry until lightly browned. Transfer to the stoneware pot.
3. Stir the paprika into the fat in the pan, then add the stock and bring to the boil, stirring. Pour over the liver and add the pimento and caraway seeds.
4. Cover and cook on Low for 6-8 hours or High for 3-4 hours. Taste and adjust the seasoning before serving.

BACON POT ROAST [S]

Serves 6
Preparation time: 10 minutes
Cooking time: High 1 hour, then
*   Low 7 hours or High 3-4 hours*

1 × 1½ kg/3 lb collar bacon joint
2 tablespoons oil
2 medium leeks, trimmed and
    cut into 5 cm/2 inch lengths
225 g/8 oz carrots,
    peeled and quartered
1 bay leaf
150 ml/¼ pint hot beef stock
salt
freshly ground black pepper

1. Soak the bacon in the cold water for several hours or overnight.
2. Heat the oil in a frying pan. Add the leeks and carrots and brown lightly. Lift out and transfer to the stoneware pot.
3. Drain the bacon joint and pat dry thoroughly with paper towels. Put into the frying pan and brown in the oil on all sides. Transfer to the stoneware pot, arranging the vegetables around it.
4. Add the bay leaf, stock and salt and pepper to taste.
5. Cover and cook on High for 1 hour, then turn to Low to cook for 7 hours, or continue cooking on High for 3-4 hours. Discard the bay leaf before serving.

KIDNEY AND VEGETABLE HOTPOT [P]

Preparation time: 15 minutes
Cooking time: H pressure 5 minutes

750 g/1½ lb lambs' kidneys
1 tablespoon oil
2 teaspoons plain flour
300 ml/½ pint beef stock
4 celery sticks, cut into 1 cm/
    ½ inch pieces
1 small swede, peeled and
    cut into 2.5 cm/1 inch cubes
1 medium parsnip, peeled and
    cut into 2.5 cm/1 inch cubes
500 g/1 lb potatoes, peeled and
    cut into 2.5 cm/1 inch cubes
1 tablespoon tomato purée
½ teaspoon dried rosemary
salt
freshly ground black pepper
chopped fresh parsley,
    to garnish

1. Skin and halve the kidneys. Remove the cores.
2. Heat the oil in the open cooker, add the kidneys and brown lightly. Lift out, draining well.
3. Stir the flour into the fat in the cooker until absorbed. Add the stock and stir well.
4. Add all the remaining ingredients to the cooker, with salt and pepper to taste, together with the kidneys. Stir to mix.
5. Close the cooker, bring to H pressure quickly.
6. Taste and adjust the seasoning. Serve garnished with a little chopped parsley, accompanied by hot French bread.

Top left: Paprika liver casserole
Top right: Sweetbreads au gratin
Bottom left: Bacon pot roast
Bottom right: Kidney and vegetable hotpot

SWEETBREADS AU GRATIN ᴾ

Preparation time: 25 minutes
Cooking time: H pressure 6 minutes

750 g/1½ lb lambs' sweetbreads
2 tablespoons cooking oil
100 g/4 oz unsmoked bacon,
  rind removed, chopped
2 celery sticks, finely chopped
1 small onion,
  peeled and finely chopped
300 ml/½ pint chicken stock
1 bouquet garni
salt
freshly ground black pepper
TO FINISH:
25 g/1 oz margarine
25 g/1 oz plain flour
150 ml/¼ pint milk
75 g/3 oz cheese, grated

1. Remove any membranes or blood vessels from the sweetbreads. Soak in several changes of cold water for 2 hours. Drain and cut into bite-sized pieces.
2. Place the sweetbreads in the cooker, cover with cold water and bring to the boil. Boil for 3 minutes, then drain and rinse with cold water.
3. Heat the oil in the cooker. Add the bacon, celery and onion and fry until softened. Lift out, draining well.
4. Add the sweetbreads to the hot oil and fry until lightly coloured.
5. Return the vegetables and bacon to the cooker with the stock, bouquet garni and salt and pepper to taste. Stir well.
6. Close the cooker, bring to H pressure and cook for 6 minutes. Reduce the pressure quickly.

7. Drain off the cooking liquid, strain and reserve. Transfer the sweetbreads to a warmed flameproof serving dish and keep hot.
8. Return the rinsed cooker to the heat and add the margarine. When melted, stir in the flour and cook for 1 minute. Remove the cooker from the heat and gradually stir in the reserved cooking liquid and the milk. Return to the heat and bring to the boil, stirring. Add 50 g/ 2 oz of the cheese and season to taste with salt and pepper.
9. Pour the sauce over the sweetbreads and sprinkle the remaining cheese on top. Brown under a hot grill. Serve with creamed potatoes.

LAMB'S KIDNEY & MUSHROOM BRAISE

Preparation time: 15 minutes
Cooking time: about 20 minutes
Oven: 150°C, 300°F, Gas Mark 2

450 g/1 lb lamb's kidneys,
    skinned, cored and halved
50 g/2 oz butter
1 tablespoon oil
2 medium onions,
    peeled and finely chopped
1 tablespoon plain flour
4 streaky bacon rashers,
    rind removed, diced
1 tablespoon sherry
150 ml/¼ pint chicken stock
1 teaspoon tomato purée
100 g/4 oz button mushrooms,
    quartered
salt
freshly ground black pepper
750 g/1½ lb potatoes, peeled
5-6 tablespoons milk
2 tablespoons diced red pepper,
    to garnish

1. Put the kidneys into a saucepan, cover with cold water and bring just to boiling point. Drain and refresh under cold running water for a few minutes. Then place in a casserole.
2. Melt 25 g/1 oz of the butter in a frying pan, add the oil and onions and cook gently until golden brown. Sprinkle with the flour and cook for 1-2 minutes, then add the bacon, sherry, stock, tomato purée, mushrooms and salt and pepper to taste.
3. Bring to the boil, stirring well, then pour over the kidneys in the casserole. Cover and cook in a preheated oven for about 20 minutes or until the kidneys are tender (test with the tip of a skewer).
4. Meanwhile, cook the potatoes in boiling water until tender. Drain well, then mash with the remaining butter, the milk and salt and pepper to taste. Spoon or pipe the potato around the edge of a flameproof dish and brown lightly under the grill.
5. Pour the kidney braise into the centre and garnish with the pepper. Serve with a green vegetable and redcurrant jelly.

LEMON HEARTS P

Preparation time. 25 minutes
Cooking time: H pressure 30 minutes

50 g/2 oz fresh white
   breadcrumbs
finely grated rind of 1-2 lemons
3 tablespoons lemon juice
50 g/2 oz mushrooms,
   finely chopped
25 g/1 oz shredded suet
salt
freshly ground black pepper
4 large lambs' hearts,
   trimmed of fat and sinew
1 tablespoon oil
600 ml/1 pint beef stock
2 teaspoons cornflour
1 tablespoon cold water

1. Mix together the breadcrumbs, lemon rind, lemon juice, mushrooms, suet and salt and pepper to taste. Fill the hearts with this stuffing and stitch together the opening with strong thread.
2. Heat the oil in the open cooker. Add the hearts and brown on all sides. Remove the cooker from the heat and add the stock and a little salt and pepper.
3. Close the cooker, bring to H pressure and cook for 30 minutes. Reduce the pressure quickly.
4. Lift out the hearts and remove the threads. Place on a heated serving dish and keep hot. Return the open cooker to the heat. Dissolve the cornflour in the cold water and add to the cooker. Bring to the boil and simmer, stirring, for 1-2 minutes. Taste and adjust the seasoning. Pour the sauce over the hearts and serve.

MOCK GOOSE

Preparation time: 35 minutes,
   plus soaking time
Cooking time: 1¾-2¼ hours
Oven: 150°C, 300°F, Gas Mark 2

2 calves' hearts or
   4 lambs' hearts
2 medium onions,
   peeled, cooked in boiling
   water
   and finely chopped
50 g/2 oz butter, softened
100 g/4 oz fresh white
   breadcrumbs
6 fresh sage leaves, finely
   chopped, or 1 teaspoon dried
   sage
½ teaspoon ground mace
salt
freshly ground black pepper
beaten egg, to mix
50 g/2 oz seasoned flour
2 tablespoons beef dripping
450 ml/¾ pint beef stock
25 g/1 oz plain flour
TO GARNISH:
4 bacon rolls, grilled
4 chipolata sausages, grilled

1. Trim the hearts and remove the tubes, arteries and any gristle. Soak in cold water for 30 minutes.
2. Drain, rinse and place in a saucepan. Cover with fresh cold water, bring to the boil, drain again and refresh under cold running water for a few minutes.
3. Mix together the onions, 25 g/1 oz of the butter, the breadcrumbs, sage and mace and season well with salt and pepper. Bind with a little beaten egg. Use to stuff the hearts and sew up with linen thread or fine string. Toss in the 50 g/2 oz seasoned flour.
4. Heat the dripping in a flameproof casserole, add the hearts and fry until lightly coloured on all sides. Sprinkle with any remaining seasoned flour, cook for 1-2 minutes and then stir in the stock. Bring to the boil.
5. Cover and cook in a preheated oven for 1¾-2 hours, or until the hearts are tender (test with a sterilized steel knitting pin or fine skewer). Lift the hearts on to a heated dish, remove the thread or string and keep hot.
6. Reduce the cooking liquid by rapid boiling over a high heat.
7. Mash together the remaining butter and 25 g/1 oz flour to make a paste. Mix in a little of the cooking liquid, then stir this into the remaining liquid. Simmer, stirring, until thickened. Adjust the seasoning.
8. Garnish the hearts with the bacon rolls and chipolatas, and serve with apple sauce and the thickened gravy.

Above: Lamb's kidney and mushroom braise

Far left: Lemon hearts
Left: Mock goose

STUFFED CHICKEN

Preparation time: 35 minutes
Cooking time: 2½ hours
Oven: 160°C, 325°F, Gas Mark 3

100 g/4 oz ribbon noodles,
    cooked and drained
75 g/3 oz soft liver pâté
3 tablespoons double cream
2 tablespoons chopped fresh
    parsley
½ teaspoon ground nutmeg
salt
freshly ground black pepper
1 × 1.5 kg/3½ lb roasting
    chicken
50 g/2 oz butter
1 tablespoon oil
2 medium onions,
    peeled and finely chopped
2 carrots, trimmed, lightly
    scraped, and finely diced
1 bay leaf
2 tablespoons sherry
300 ml/½ pint chicken stock
1 teaspoon arrowroot
TO GARNISH:
whole baked tomatoes
sprigs of watercress

1. To make the stuffing, mix together the noodles, liver pâté, cream, parsley and nutmeg, and season with salt and pepper.
2. Wipe the inside of the chicken with a clean damp cloth, then stuff it. Sew, if necessary, and truss.
3. Melt the butter with the oil in a flameproof casserole, add the chicken and brown carefully on all sides.
4. Lift the chicken on to a dish. Add the onions and carrots to the casserole and cook gently for 5 minutes.
5. Add the bay leaf and sherry and allow to bubble for 2 minutes.
6. Place the chicken on top of the vegetables, season lightly with salt and pepper and pour the stock around the sides. Cover and cook in a preheated oven, basting from time to time for 2 hours.
7. Remove the lid and continue cooking, uncovered, for about 30 minutes or until the chicken is tender and the sauce reduced.
8. Lift the chicken into a heated serving dish. Dissolve the arrowroot in a little stock or water.

9. Skim the fat from the sauce. Remove the bay leaf. Bring the sauce to the boil on top of the stove, stir in the arrowroot and bring just to the boil again. Adjust the seasoning. Pour into a heated sauceboat.
10. Garnish the chicken with tomatoes and watercress, and serve with Braised Celery (page 99).

STUFFED CHICKEN DRUMSTICKS

Preparation time: 30 minutes
Cooking time: 1½ hours
Oven 160°C, 325°F, Gas Mark 3

100 g/4 oz shredded suet
50 g/2 oz cooked ham,
    finely chopped
100 g/4 oz fresh breadcrumbs
15 g/½ oz fresh parsley,
    finely chopped
1 teaspoon finely chopped fresh
    marjoram, or
    ½ teaspoon dried marjoram
grated rind of 1 lemon
25 g/1 oz blanched almonds,
    chopped
2 eggs, beaten
salt
freshly ground black pepper
8 chicken drumsticks
50 g/2 oz seasoned flour
3 tablespoons oil
2 medium onions,
    peeled and finely chopped
450 g/1 lb carrots,
    trimmed, scraped and sliced
450 ml/¾ pint chicken stock
2 teaspoons cornflour (optional)
2 tablespoons sherry (optional)
TO GARNISH:
fried bread triangles
chopped fresh parsley

1. To make the stuffing, mix together the suet, ham, breadcrumbs, parsley, marjoram, lemon rind, almonds and beaten eggs and season to taste with salt and pepper.
2. With a very sharp small knife, carefully cut around the flesh at the top of each drumstick, then gently scrape the flesh away from the bone down to the claw end, turning as you do so. (Once you have freed the tip of the bone, it is easy.)
3. Using kitchen paper to get a grip, pull the flesh and bone apart. Turn the drumsticks back to their original shape.
4. Divide the stuffing equally between the drumsticks, pushing it well down into the cavity left by the bone. Close up the skin and sew with linen or fine thread.
5. Use the seasoned flour to coat the drumsticks.
6. Heat the oil in a large frying pan, add the drumsticks and brown lightly all over. Transfer to a casserole.
7. Add the onions and carrots to the frying pan and cook gently for 5 minutes. Add to the drumsticks. Bring the stock to the boil in the frying pan, scraping up the sediment. Adjust the seasoning and pour into the casserole. Cover and cook in a preheated oven for 1 hour.
8. Remove the lid, baste the chicken with

the sauce and return the casserole to the oven uncovered. Continue cooking for 30 minutes or until the sauce has reduced and the chicken is tender and golden.
9. If a thickened sauce is preferred, transfer the chicken and vegetables to a heated serving dish and keep hot. Pour the sauce into a saucepan.
10. Dissolve the cornflour in the sherry and add to the pan. Bring to the boil, stirring constantly, and simmer for 2 minutes. Adjust the seasoning. Pour the sauce over the chicken, and garnish with fried bread and parsley.

Above left: Stuffed chicken drumsticks
Above right: Stuffed chicken

Right: Pot au feu

POT AU FEU

Preparation time: 30 minutes,
plus soaking time
Cooking time: 3½ hours
Oven: 150℃, 300°F, Gas Mark 2

450 g/1 lb shin of beef,
  trimmed and cut into 7.5 cm/
  3 inch pieces
1 oxtail, cut into 5 cm/2 inch
  pieces and soaked in cold
  water for 1 hour
2 chicken legs,
  preferably from a boiling fowl
2 onions, peeled and left whole
3 carrots,
  scraped and thickly sliced
2 leeks, white part only,
  thickly sliced
½ small turnip,
  peeled and sliced
1 stick celery, sliced
1 bouquet garni
2.25 litres/4 pints light beef
  stock
salt
1 × 15 cm/6 inch length of beef
  marrow bone, tied in muslin
  (optional)
freshly ground black pepper
4 thick slices bread,
  cut from a French bread stick
creamed horseradish

This recipe is an adaptation of the classic French Pot au Feu, which may also include pork or sausage. In this version, the meat and vegetables are served with the highly flavoured broth, whereas in France the broth is usually one dish and the meat and vegetables another. Apart from the French bread and horseradish suggested here other accompaniments include freshly boiled potatoes and pickled cucumber.

1. Put the beef, oxtail and chicken legs into a large saucepan. Cover with plenty of cold water and bring very slowly to the boil, skimming off the scum as it rises. Simmer for 5 minutes, skimming constantly, then drain.
2. Put the beef and oxtail into a deep casserole; reserve the chicken legs. Add the onions, carrots, leeks, turnip, celery, bouquet garni, beef stock and a little salt to the casserole. Cover and cook in a preheated oven for 2½ hours.
3. Add the chicken legs and marrow bone, cover and cook for 1 hour.
4. Lift out the marrow bone, oxtail, chicken legs, onions and bouquet garni.
5. Scoop the marrow from the bone and reserve. Remove the meat from the oxtail and chicken legs and return it to the casserole.
6. Discard the onions and bouquet garni. Skim the fat off the broth and adjust the seasoning. Reheat gently in the oven.
7. Toast the bread to deep golden brown. Spread 4 of the slices with the reserved marrow and a little creamed horseradish.
8. Serve the soup in deep bowls accompanied by the toast.

TURKEY MEXICANA

Preparation time: 20 minutes
Cooking time: 1 hour
Oven: 160°C, 325°F, Gas Mark 3

50 g/2 oz seasoned flour
4 turkey fillets
3 tablespoons oil
1 medium onion,
    peeled and thinly sliced
1 small red pepper,
    cored, seeded and sliced
300 ml/½ pint chicken stock
25 g/1 oz seedless raisins
pinch of ground cloves
pinch of ground cumin
½ teaspoon ground cinnamon
3 tomatoes,
    skinned, seeded and sliced
1 teaspoon chilli powder
1 tablespoon sesame seeds
salt
freshly ground black pepper
25 g/1 oz plain dark chocolate,
    grated
TO GARNISH:
lime or lemon wedges
4 sprigs parsley or coriander
    leaves

Chilli powder is very hot and varies in strength according to the brand used, so use it cautiously.

1. Use the seasoned flour to coat the turkey fillets.
2. Heat the oil in a frying pan, add the turkey and cook until lightly browned. Transfer to a casserole.
3. Add the onion and red pepper to the frying pan and cook gently until they begin to soften. Sprinkle in any remaining seasoned flour and cook for 2-3 minutes.
4. Stir in the stock, raisins, cloves, cumin, cinnamon, tomatoes, chilli powder, sesame seeds and chocolate. Season lightly with salt and pepper. Bring to the boil and simmer for 10 minutes.
5. Pour the sauce over the turkey. Cover the casserole and cook in a preheated oven for 50 minutes. Adjust the seasoning, then garnish with lime or lemon and parsley or coriander.
6. Serve with sweetcorn and green beans.

SMOKY CHICKEN PARCELS S

Preparation time: 25 minutes
Cooking time: Low 6-8 hours
    High 3 hours

8 smoked streaky bacon rashers,
    rind removed
50 g/2 oz mushrooms,
    finely chopped
½ teaspoon dried basil
salt
freshly ground black pepper
8 chicken drumsticks, skinned
1 tablespoon oil
1 × 425 g/15 oz can cream of
    mushroom soup
2 teaspoons cornflour
1 tablespoon cold water
chopped fresh parsley,
    to garnish

1. Using a round-bladed knife spread and stretch the bacon rashers on a board until they are approximately doubled in size.
2. Mix together the mushrooms, basil and salt and pepper to taste. Spread this over the bacon rashers, pressing it down well.
3. Place a chicken drumstick at one end of a rasher of bacon and carefully roll up so that the drumstick is fully encased in bacon. Secure the end with a wooden cocktail stick.
4. Heat the oil in a frying pan. Add the chicken parcels and cook until lightly browned on all sides. Transfer to the stoneware pot.
5. Spread the soup evenly over the chicken.
6. Cover and cook on Low for 6-8 hours or High for 3 hours.
7. Remove the chicken parcels. Remove the cocktail sticks, then set aside and keep hot. Dissolve the cornflour in the cold water and stir into the sauce until it has thickened. Taste and adjust the seasoning. Return the chicken to the sauce and reheat thoroughly.
8. Serve sprinkled with a little chopped parsley.

CHICKEN CASSEROLE

Preparation time: 15 minutes
Cooking time: 40 minutes
Oven: 180°C, 350°F, Gas Mark 4

25 g/1 oz butter
350 g/12 oz boneless chicken
 breasts, skinned and cut into
 strips
100 g/4 oz French beans,
 sliced into 5 cm/2 inch
 lengths
1 stick celery, very thinly sliced
25 g/1 oz walnuts,
 coarsely chopped
2 tomatoes,
 skinned, seeded and sliced
½ green pepper,
 cored, seeded and thinly
 sliced
½ red pepper,
 cored, seeded and thinly
 sliced
2 dessert apples,
 peeled, cored and sliced
600 ml/1 pint medium dry cider
salt
freshly ground black pepper
1 tablespoon cornflour,
 dissolved in a little cider
2 teaspoons chopped fresh mint,
 to garnish

1. Melt the butter in a flameproof
casserole. When foaming add the chicken
strips and fry, stirring, for 3-4 minutes
just to stiffen, not to colour.
2. Add the beans, celery, walnuts,
tomatoes, peppers and apples. Mix well
and pour in the cider. Season with salt
and pepper.
3. Bring to the boil, then cover and cook
in a preheated oven for 35 minutes.
4. Remove the lid, stir in the cornflour
and bring carefully to boiling point on top
of the stove, stirring. Remove from the
heat immediately.
5. Garnish with the chopped mint and
serve with croquette potatoes and
buttered courgettes.

QUICK CHICKEN HASH

Preparation time: 15 minutes
Cooking time: 35 minutes
Oven: 180°C, 350°F, Gas Mark 4

450 g/1 lb cooked chicken meat,
 diced
1 × 225 g/8 oz packet frozen
 peas, thawed
50 g/2 oz blanched almonds,
 slivered
6 black olives,
 stoned and finely chopped
1 × 275 g/10 oz can condensed
 cream of mushroom soup
1 small red pepper,
 cored, seeded and diced
salt
freshly ground black pepper
TO GARNISH:
3 tablespoons Fried Croûtons
 (page 141)
sprig of watercress

1. Mix together the chicken, peas,
almonds and olives.
2. Heat the undiluted soup in a small
pan, then stir it into the chicken mixture
together with the red pepper. Add salt
and pepper to taste. Pour into a casserole,
cover and cook in a preheated oven for 35
minutes.
3. Garnish with croûtons and watercress
and serve with saffron rice.

Top left: Turkey mexicana
Top right: Chicken casserole
Bottom left: Smoky chicken parcels
Bottom right: Quick chicken hash

FISH STEW PROVENÇALE

Preparation time: 20 minutes
Cooking time: 25 minutes
Oven: 180°C, 350°F, Gas Mark 4

2 tablespoons olive oil
100 g/4 oz shallots,
    peeled and thinly sliced
2 garlic cloves,
    peeled and crushed
120 ml/4 fl oz dry white wine
300 ml/½ pint fish stock
pinch of cayenne
salt
freshly ground black pepper
1 bouquet garni
large pinch of saffron powder
1 kg/2 lb mixed white,
    firm-fleshed fish (huss, hake,
    witch, cod), skinned and cut
    into 2 inch pieces
2 teaspoons cornflour
3 tablespoons double cream
    (optional)
few cooked mussels in half
    shell, to garnish

1. Heat the oil in a flameproof casserole, add the shallots and cook gently until soft and golden brown. Add the garlic and white wine, bring to the boil and allow to bubble until reduced by half.
2. Stir in the stock and cayenne, season lightly with salt and pepper and add the bouquet garni and saffron. Place the fish in the casserole, cover and cook in a preheated oven for 20 minutes.
3. Lift the fish pieces carefully into a heated dish and keep hot. Reduce the sauce by boiling for 5 minutes.
4. Dissolve the cornflour in a little fish stock or water and add to the sauce. Simmer, stirring, until thickened. Adjust the seasoning. Stir in the cream.
5. Return the fish to the sauce and reheat gently. Do not allow to boil.
6. Garnish with mussels, and serve with plenty of Hot Garlic Bread (page 140).

Right: Fish stew provençale

MIXED FISH CASSEROLE WITH MUSTARD CREAM

Preparation time: 20 minutes
Cooking time: 35 minutes
Oven: 160°C, 325°F, Gas Mark 3

50 g/2 oz butter
3 medium onions,
    peeled and finely chopped
2 garlic cloves,
    peeled and crushed
1 bouquet garni
2 cloves
150 ml/¼ pint dry white wine
150 ml/¼ pint fish stock or very
    light chicken stock
juice of ½ lemon
salt
freshly ground black pepper
750 g/1¾ lb mixed white fish
    fillets (plaice, cod, haddock,
    lemon sole, huss, whiting),
    skinned and cut into 5 cm/
    2 inch pieces
100 g/4 oz button mushrooms,
    sliced
100 g/4 oz fresh or frozen peas
1 teaspoon Dijon mustard
4 tablespoons double cream
TO GARNISH:
puff pastry crescents
sprigs of watercress

1. Melt the butter in a frying pan, add the onions and fry gently until softened.
2. Stir in the garlic, bouquet garni, cloves, white wine and stock. Bring to the boil and simmer for 5 minutes. Allow to cool slightly, then pour into a casserole. Stir in the lemon juice and salt and pepper to taste and add the fish pieces.
3. Cover and cook in a preheated oven for 25 minutes.
4. Add the mushrooms and peas and continue cooking for 10 minutes. Discard the bouquet garni.
5. Stir the mustard into the cream and stir into the casserole carefully – do not break the fish. Adjust the seasoning.
6. Garnish with pastry fleurons and watercress, and serve with sauté potatoes and mange tout peas.

Right: Mixed fish casserole with mustard cream
Far right: Seafood casserole

SEAFOOD CASSEROLE

Preparation time: 50 minutes
Cooking time: 50 minutes
Oven: 180°C, 350°F, Gas Mark 4
*   200°C, 400°F, Gas Mark 6*

225 g/8 oz cod fillet, skinned
    and cut into 5 cm/2 inch
    pieces
225 g/8 oz huss, cut into 5 cm/
    2 inch lengths
4 scallops, opened and cleaned
4 oz fresh or frozen crab meat
300 ml/½ pint hot Parsley Sauce
    (page 81)
2 teaspoons chopped fresh dill or
    ½ teaspoon dried dill
salt
freshly ground black pepper
2 tablespoons tomato purée
750 g/1½ lb creamed potato
50 g/2 oz Cheddar cheese,
    grated
TO GARNISH:
few unpeeled prawns
chopped parsley

1. Arrange the cod, huss and scallops in a casserole.
2. Stir the crab meat into the parsley sauce, add the dill and taste and adjust the seasoning. Mix well together, pour over the fish, cover and cook in a preheated oven for 30 minutes.
3. Meanwhile, beat the tomato purée into the creamed potato. Taste and adjust the seasoning.
4. Remove the lid from the casserole, raise the oven temperature, pipe or spoon the potato over the fish, leaving a space in the centre, into which sprinkle the cheese.
5. Return the dish to the oven for about 20 minutes, uncovered, until golden and bubbling. Do not leave it to cook any longer as this will toughen the scallops. Garnish with prawns and parsley.

SMOKED MACKEREL RAMEKINS

Preparation time: 10 minutes
Cooking time: 25 minutes
Oven: 180°C, 350°F, Gas Mark 4

350 g/12 oz smoked mackerel
  fillets, skinned and flaked
1 small onion, peeled and grated
300 ml/½ pint single cream
salt
freshly ground black pepper
1 tablespoon creamed
  horseradish
4 tablespoons Seasoned Crumbs
  (page 140)

1. Mix together the fish, onion and cream. Season carefully with salt and pepper. Stir in the horseradish (more may be added if liked).
2. Divide the mixture between four ramekins and cover each one with foil.
3. Cook in a preheated oven for 15 minutes, then remove the foil, sprinkle 1 tablespoon of the seasoned crumbs over each dish and return to the oven.
4. Bake for a further 10 minutes or until golden and bubbling.

SMOKED HADDOCK SPECIAL

Preparation time: 30 minutes
Cooking time: 40 minutes
Oven: 160°C, 325°F, Gas Mark 3

750 g/2 lb smoked haddock
  fillets, skinned and halved
2 teaspoons lemon juice
salt
freshly ground black pepper
25 g/1 oz butter
1 medium onion,
  peeled and finely chopped
150 ml/¼ pint milk
1 bay leaf
1 tablespoon cornflour
150 ml/¼ pint single cream
1 × 225 g/8 oz packet frozen
  mixed vegetables (including
  sweetcorn), thawed
2 tablespoons chopped fresh
  parsley
50 g/2 oz Cheddar cheese,
  grated
skinned tomato slices, to garnish

1. Place the fish in a flameproof casserole, pour over the lemon juice and season with salt and pepper.
2. Melt the butter in a small frying pan, add the onion and fry until softened.
3. Pour the onion over the fish and add the milk and bay leaf. Cover and cook in a preheated oven for 20 minutes.
4. Remove the bay leaf. Dissolve the cornflour in the cream and pour into the casserole.
5. Bring to the boil on top of the stove, stirring gently to avoid breaking up the fish. Remove from the heat.
6. Add the vegetables and parsley and mix carefully. Adjust the seasoning. Sprinkle the cheese over the top.
7. Return to the oven and bake for a further 20 minutes or until the vegetables are cooked and the cheese topping golden brown.
8. Garnish with tomato slices and serve with new potatoes, dressed with parsley, butter and lemon juice, and sautéed cucumber slices.

ORANGE MACKEREL BAKE   [S]

Preparation time: 15 minutes
Cooking time: Low 4-6 hours
  High 2-3 hours

50 g/2 oz fresh white
  breadcrumbs
finely grated rind of 2 oranges
4 tablespoons orange juice
1 small onion, peeled and grated
½ teaspoon dried dill
salt
freshly ground black pepper
4 medium mackerel,
  cleaned and boned
150 ml/¼ pint hot chicken stock
1 tablespoon chopped fresh
  parsley

1. Mix together the breadcrumbs, orange rind and juice, onion, dill and salt and pepper to taste.
2. Lay the mackerel on a board, skin side down. Divide the stuffing between the fish and spread almost to the edges. Roll up from the head end and secure with wooden cocktail sticks.
3. Place the fish rolls in the stoneware pot. Pour over the stock and sprinkle with the chopped parsley.
4. Cover and cook on Low for 4-6 hours or High for 2-3 hours.
5. Remove the cocktail sticks, and serve with plain boiled potatoes or crisp French bread.

PIGEONS WITH APRICOTS

Preparation time: 30 minutes,
plus soaking time
Cooking time: 1½ hours
Oven: 160℃, 325°F, Gas Mark 3

50 g/2 oz butter
4 young pigeons, trussed,
  livers reserved
2 onions,
  peeled and finely chopped
150 ml/¼ pint dry white wine
150 ml/¼ pint giblet or chicken
  stock
225 g/8 oz dried apricots,
  soaked in water overnight
1 teaspoon chopped fresh
  tarragon or ½ teaspoon dried
  tarragon
salt
freshly ground black pepper
2 tablespoons Amaretto di
  Sarronno
1 teaspoon arrowroot
TO GARNISH:
flaked almonds, toasted
sprigs of watercress

1. Melt the butter in a large frying pan, add the pigeons and brown all over. Transfer to a casserole.
2. Stir the onions into the butter in the frying pan and cook gently until golden. Pour in the wine, bring to the boil and allow to reduce a little.
3. Stir in the stock, drained apricots and tarragon. Season to taste with salt and pepper. Bring to the boil, then pour over the pigeons in the casserole.
4. Cover and cook in a preheated oven for 1 hour 10 minutes or until the birds are tender.
5. Lift the pigeons on to a board. Cut away the trussing string, then arrange them on a heated serving dish with the apricots. Keep hot.
6. Slice the reserved livers. Pour the sauce into a saucepan, add the livers, and gently simmer for 2-3 minutes.
7. Dissolve the arrowroot in a little cold water and stir into the sauce with the Amaretto. Bring to the boil, stirring until thickened. Adjust the seasoning. Pour the sauce over the pigeons, and garnish with almonds and watercress.

PHEASANT IN RED WINE

Preparation time: 30 minutes,
  plus cooking chestnuts
Cooking time: 1 hour
Oven: 180℃, 350°F, Gas Mark 4

½ bottle dry red wine
25 g/1 oz butter
1 × 1½ kg/3 lb young pheasant,
  jointed, liver reserved
1 onion, peeled and sliced
1 carrot, peeled and sliced
1 garlic clove,
  peeled and crushed
25 g/1 oz plain flour
sprig of fresh rosemary or
  ½ teaspoon dried rosemary
150 ml/¼ pint giblet or chicken
  stock
salt
freshly ground black pepper
225 g/8 oz chestnuts,
  peeled and cooked
TO GARNISH:
15 g/½ oz butter
4 × 5 cm/2 inch rounds fried
  bread
chopped fresh parsley

1. Pour the wine into a small saucepan, bring to the boil and simmer until reduced by half. Remove from the heat and reserve.
2. Melt the butter in a frying pan, add the pheasant joints and brown on all sides. Transfer to a casserole.
3. Add the onion and carrot to the frying pan and cook gently for 5 minutes. Add to the casserole with the garlic.
4. Stir the flour into the fat in the frying pan and cook for 2 minutes. Stir in the reserved reduced wine, the rosemary and stock and bring to the boil, stirring. Season to taste with salt and pepper.
5. Pour the sauce over the pheasant in the casserole, then cover and cook in a preheated oven for 45 minutes.
6. Add the chestnuts and cook for a further 15 minutes.
7. Meanwhile for the garnish, slice the pheasant liver. Melt the butter in a small pan, add the liver and cook for 4 minutes. Remove from the heat and pound to a smooth cream. Season with salt and pepper and spread on the fried bread. Dust with parsley.
8. Garnish the pheasant with the bread rounds, and serve with creamed potato and braised red cabbage.

COQ AU VIN

Preparation time: 40 minutes
Cooking time: 1½ hours
Oven: 180°C, 350°F, Gas Mark 4

45 g/1¾ oz butter
100 g/4 oz thick unsmoked
   streaky bacon, rind removed,
   blanched and diced
12 pickling onions, peeled
1 × 1½ kg/3 lb roasting chicken,
   jointed
2 tablespoons brandy
1 bottle Burgundy
salt
freshly ground black pepper
2 garlic cloves,
   peeled and crushed
1 bouquet garni
½ teaspoon ground nutmeg
225 g/8 oz small button
   mushrooms
20 g/¾ oz plain flour
1 teaspoon meat extract
   (optional)
TO GARNISH:
heart-shaped Fried Croûtons
   (page 141)
chopped fresh parsley

1. Melt 25 g/1 oz of the butter in a flameproof casserole, add the bacon and onions and cook gently until the onions begin to colour. Transfer to a plate.
2. Add the chicken joints to the casserole and brown on all sides.
3. Warm the brandy, pour it over the chicken and set alight.
4. When the flames die down, replace the bacon and onions in the casserole.
5. Heat the wine in a saucepan and pour over the chicken. Season to taste with salt and pepper. Stir in the garlic, bouquet garni and nutmeg. Cover the casserole and cook in a preheated oven for 1 hour.
6. Stir in the mushrooms, re-cover and cook for a further 15 minutes. Remove the bouquet garni.
7. Mix the flour with the remaining butter to a paste and whisk into the sauce in small pieces. Bring just to the boil, stirring.
8. Stir in the beef and yeast extract, if using – this deepens the colour; red wine sauces tend to have an unappetizing 'greyness'. Adjust the seasoning, and garnish with croûtons and parsley.

Far left: Pheasant in red wine
Left: Coq au vin

POUSSINS IN SHERRY   S

Preparation time: 12 minutes
Cooking time: Low 7-9 hours
*   High 3-4 hours*

50 g/2 oz butter
4 poussins, trussed
100 g/4 oz pork chipolatas
4 unsmoked streaky bacon
   rashers, rind removed,
   chopped
100 g/4 oz mushrooms
150 ml/¼ pint medium dry
   sherry
salt
freshly ground black pepper
TO FINISH:
1 tablespoon cornflour
2 tablespoons medium dry
   sherry
1 tablespoon chopped fresh
   chives

1. Melt the butter in a frying pan. Add the poussins and brown on all sides. Transfer to the stoneware pot.
2. Divide the chipolatas into two by twisting and then cutting in half. Add these to the frying pan with the bacon. Fry until both are lightly browned. Arrange around the poussins in the stoneware pot.
3. Add the mushrooms to the frying pan with the sherry and salt and pepper to taste. Bring to the boil, then pour over the ingredients in the stoneware pot.
4. Cover and cook on Low for 7-9 hours or High for 3-4 hours.
5. Lift out the poussins and remove the strings. Keep hot. Dissolve the cornflour in the sherry and stir into the sauce until it has thickened. Taste and adjust the seasoning. Return the poussins to the sauce, baste well and reheat. Sprinkle with the chopped chives and serve.

Left: Poussins in sherry

CHICKEN WITH ARTICHOKES

Preparation time: 1½ hours
Cooking time: 35 minutes
Oven: 180°C, 350°F, Gas Mark 4
*   200°C, 400°F, Gas Mark 6*

1 × 1½ kg/3 lb roasting chicken, trussed
600 ml/1 pint chicken stock
50 g/2 oz butter
50 g/2 oz shallots, peeled and finely chopped
1 garlic clove, peeled and crushed
40 g/1½ oz plain flour
4 tablespoons dry white wine
150 ml/¼ pint double cream
1 teaspoon Dijon mustard
1 teaspoon chopped fresh tarragon, or ½ teaspoon dried tarragon
1 × 425 g/15 oz can artichoke hearts, drained and quartered
salt
freshly ground black pepper
100 g/4 oz Cheese Straw Pastry (page 140) (optional)
spray of fresh tarragon, to garnish

1. Place the chicken in a flameproof casserole, pour in the stock and bring slowly to the boil over gentle heat. Cover and simmer for 1 hour.
2. Leave the chicken to cool a little in the stock, then transfer it to a board. Reserve the stock.
3. Strip off the chicken skin. Keeping the breast meat whole, remove all the meat from the bones and arrange in a shallow earthenware casserole. Slice each breast in half and lay on top.
4. Melt the butter in a saucepan, add the shallots and cook gently until softened. Stir in the garlic and flour and cook for 2-3 minutes.
5. Skim the fat from the stock, measure 150 ml/¼ pint and gradually stir it into the saucepan together with the wine, cream, mustard and tarragon. Stirring constantly, bring to the boil, then add the artichokes. Season to taste with salt and pepper.
6. Pour the sauce over the chicken, cover the casserole and cook in a preheated oven for 20 minutes.
7. Meanwhile, roll out the cheese pastry thinly and cut into narrow strips. Remove the lid of the casserole, raise the oven temperature and arrange the pastry strips in a lattice over the chicken. Cook for a further 15 minutes or until the pastry is crisp and golden.
8. Garnish with tarragon. Use the remaining stock for soup.

CHICKEN MARENGO

Preparation time: 25 minutes
Cooking time: 1¼ hours
Oven: 180°C, 350°F, Gas Mark 4

40 g/1½ oz seasoned flour
1 × 1½ kg/3 lb roasting chicken, jointed
2 tablespoons oil
2 onions, peeled and finely chopped
150 ml/¼ pint dry white wine
150 ml/¼ pint strong chicken stock
salt
freshly ground black pepper
1 bouquet garni
100 g/4 oz mushrooms, sliced
3 tomatoes, skinned, seeded and diced
1 teaspoon tomato purée
pinch of sugar
TO GARNISH:
4 large unpeeled prawns
sprigs of parsley

1. Use the seasoned flour to coat the chicken joints.
2. Heat the oil in a frying pan, add the chicken and fry until golden on all sides. Transfer to a casserole.
3. Stir the onions into the oil in the frying pan and cook gently until soft and golden.
4. Mix in any remaining seasoned flour and continue cooking for 2-3 minutes.
5. Stir in the wine and stock and bring to the boil, then pour over the chicken in the casserole. Season to taste with salt and pepper and tuck in the bouquet garni. Cover and cook in a preheated oven for 1 hour.
6. Remove the bouquet garni and add the mushrooms, tomatoes, tomato purée and sugar. Adjust the seasoning.
7. Re-cover and continue cooking for 15 minutes.
8. Garnish with prawns and parsley, and serve with sauté potatoes and broad beans in a cream sauce.

POULET CITRON

P

*Preparation time: 10 minutes,
plus marinating time*
Cooking time: H pressure 6 minutes

4 chicken breasts, skinned
1 garlic clove,
    peeled and crushed
1 medium onion,
    peeled and chopped
finely grated rind and juice of
    1-2 lemons
1 tablespoon chopped fresh
    parsley
2 tablespoons olive oil
salt
freshly ground black pepper
50 g/2 oz butter or margarine
300 ml/½ pint chicken stock
1 tablespoon plain flour
TO GARNISH:
1 lemon, cut into wedges
1 teaspoon chopped fresh
    parsley

1. Put the chicken, garlic, onion, lemon rind and juice, parsley, oil and salt and pepper to taste into a large bowl. Cover and leave to marinate for at least 4 hours. Stir the ingredients once during this time.
2. Melt 25 g/1 oz of the butter or margarine in the open cooker. Strain off the marinade liquid and reserve. Add the chicken breasts and vegetables to the cooker and brown lightly on all sides.
3. Add the marinade liquid, stock and salt and pepper to taste and stir well.
4. Close the cooker, bring to H pressure and cook for 6 minutes. Reduce the pressure quickly.
5. Lift out the chicken, place it on a heated serving dish and keep hot. Return the open cooker to the heat. Mix the remaining butter with the flour to make a paste and stir into the sauce in small pieces. Cook, stirring, until the sauce thickens. Taste and adjust the seasoning.
6. Pour the sauce over the chicken and garnish with the lemon wedges and a little chopped parsley.

POACHED CHICKEN WITH SAUCE SUPREME

Preparation time: 30 minutes
Cooking time: 1¼ hours

1 × 1½ kg/3½ lb roasting
    chicken, trussed
900 ml/1½ pints light chicken
    stock
2 strips lemon rind, free of pith
1 tablespoon lemon juice
1 teaspoon black peppercorns
1 bouquet garni
40 g/1½ oz butter
40 g/1½ oz plain flour
½ teaspoon ground nutmeg
150 ml/¼ pint double cream
salt
freshly ground black pepper
TO GARNISH:
blanched lemon rind shreds
small cooked carrots
chopped fresh parsley

Correct reduction of the stock is essential in this recipe to produce a rich, well-flavoured sauce.

1. Place the chicken in a large flameproof casserole with the stock, lemon rind and juice, peppercorns and bouquet garni. Bring slowly to the boil. Cover and poach for 1 hour or until tender.
2. Allow to cool a little in the stock, then lift the bird carefully on to a board.
3. Strain the stock, skim off the fat and pour back into the casserole.
4. Reduce by rapid boiling to about 300 ml/½ pint.
5. Meanwhile, remove the skin from the chicken. Place the bird in a heated serving dish and keep hot.
6. Melt the butter in a saucepan, stir in the flour and cook for 2-3 minutes. Gradually stir in the reduced stock and bring to the boil. Simmer for 5 minutes, stirring, then add the nutmeg and cream. Season to taste with salt and pepper and heat through gently.
7. Pour the sauce over the chicken. Garnish the breast with lemon rind shreds, place the carrots at either end and dust them with parsley.
8. Serve with braised rice and plain boiled vegetables.

**Top: Chicken with artichokes
Centre left: Chicken marengo
Centre right: Poulet citron
Bottom: Poached chicken
with sauce supreme**

CHICKEN IN CIDER CREAM SAUCE $\boxed{S}$

Preparation time: 10 minutes
Cooking time: Low 7-9 hours
   High 3½-4 hours

2 tablespoons oil
100 g/4 oz shallots,
   peeled and sliced
4 chicken portions
100 g/4 oz mushrooms, sliced
salt
freshly ground black pepper
1 cooking apple, peeled, cored
   and cut into 4 thick slices
300 ml/½ pint dry cider
TO FINISH:
1 tablespoon cornflour
1½ tablespoons water
4 tablespoons single cream

1. Heat the oil in a frying pan. Add the shallots and brown lightly. Transfer to the stoneware pot, draining well.
2. Add the chicken portions to the frying pan and brown on all sides.
3. Add the mushrooms to the shallots in the stoneware pot and lay the browned chicken on top. Season well with salt and pepper.
4. Put the apple slices in the frying pan and brown lightly on both sides. Lay one on top of each piece of chicken. Pour the cider evenly over the chicken portions.
5. Cover and cook on Low for 7-9 hours or High for 3-4 hours.
6. Remove two of the chicken portions. Dissolve the cornflour in the water and stir into the sauce with the cream until thickened. Taste and adjust the seasoning. Return the chicken and baste all the portions with the sauce. Reheat thoroughly before serving.

LEMON PORK $\boxed{S}$

Preparation time: 20 minutes
Cooking time: Low 6-8 hours
   High 3-4 hours

2 pork fillets
salt
freshly ground black pepper
50 g/2 oz fresh white
   breadcrumbs
finely grated rind of 1 lemon
2 tablespoons lemon juice
1 tablespoon cooking oil
1 teaspoon dried sage
50 g/2 oz butter
1 medium onion,
   peeled and chopped
300 ml/½ pint dry white wine
TO FINISH:
25 g/1 oz butter
1 tablespoon plain flour

1. Trim the pork fillets of any excess fat. Lay on a board and, using a sharp knife, slice almost in half lengthways. Open each fillet out flat and flatten a little more by beating with a rolling pin or meat mallet. Season with salt and pepper.
2. Mix together the breadcrumbs, lemon rind and juice, oil and sage. Spread evenly over each fillet. Fold back in half and secure at 2.5 cm/1 inch intervals with string.
3. Melt the butter in a frying pan. Add the stuffed fillets with the onion and brown lightly on all sides.
4. Transfer the fillets and onion to the stoneware pot and add the wine.
5. Cover and cook on Low for 6-8 hours or High for 3-4 hours.
6. Thirty minutes before serving, lift out the meat and remove the strings.
7. Mix the butter with the flour to make a paste. Add in small pieces to the sauce, stirring well, and cook until thickened. Taste and adjust the seasoning. Return the meat and baste well with the sauce. Reheat thoroughly before serving.
8. Serve the meat, sliced thickly, on a bed of plain boiled rice.

Top left: Chicken in cider cream sauce
Top right: Orange and port wine gammon
Bottom left: Lemon pork
Bottom right: Turkey Veronique

ORANGE AND PORT WINE GAMMON   P

Serves 6
Preparation time: 5 minutes
Cooking time: H pressure 24 minutes

1 × 1½ kg/3 lb piece of middle
   gammon
600 ml/1 pint canned orange
   juice
2 bay leaves
TO FINISH:
150 ml/¼ pint port
1 tablespoon arrowroot
1½ tablespoons cold water
2 oranges,
   peeled and thinly sliced
few sprigs of watercress

1. Place the gammon in the cooker and add sufficient cold water to cover. Bring to the boil in the open cooker, then drain and discard the water.
2. Add the orange juice to the cooker with the bay leaves.
3. Close the cooker, bring to H pressure and cook for 24 minutes. Reduce the pressure quickly.
4. Lift out the gammon and leave to 'set' for a few minutes while making the sauce.
5. Pour 300 ml/½ pint of the cooking liquid into a jug and reserve; discard the remainder, and the bay leaves.
6. Pour the reserved cooking liquid back into the cooker, add the port and return to the heat. Dissolve the arrowroot in the water and add to the liquid. Bring to the boil, stirring until thickened. Season to taste with salt and pepper. Turn off the heat.
7. Add the orange slices to the sauce and leave to heat through while carving the gammon.
8. Carve the gammon into thick slices and arrange, overlapping, on a warmed serving dish. Pour over the sauce and garnish with a little watercress.

TURKEY VERONIQUE   P

Preparation time: 15 minutes
Cooking time: H pressure 12 minutes

50 g/2 oz butter
4 shallots or 1 small onion,
   peeled and sliced
4 turkey portions, skinned
150 ml/¼ pint chicken stock
150 ml/¼ pint dry white wine
few sprigs of parsley
175 g/6 oz green grapes, halved
   and seeded
salt
freshly ground black pepper
TO FINISH:
25 g/1 oz butter
1 tablespoon plain flour
4 tablespoons single cream

1. Melt the butter in the open cooker. Add the shallots or onion and the turkey and fry until the turkey is lightly browned on all sides.
2. Add the stock, wine, parsley, half of the grapes and salt and pepper to taste.
3. Close the cooker, bring to H pressure and cook for 12 minutes. Reduce the pressure quickly.
4. Lift out the turkey and keep hot. Discard the parsley.
5. Mix the butter with the flour to make a paste. Stir into the cooking liquid in small pieces and cook stirring constantly, until the sauce thickens. Add the remaining grapes and cook for 2 minutes. Stir in the cream. Taste and adjust the seasoning. Pour the sauce over the turkey.
Note: If using turkey breasts for this recipe, reduce the cooking time to 8 minutes.

PORK PIPPIN

Preparation time: 25 minutes
Cooking time: 1¾ hours
Oven: 160°C, 325°F, Gas Mark 3

50 g/2 oz seasoned flour
750 g/1½ lb boned pork spare rib,
    rind removed, cubed
50 g/2 oz butter
175 g/6 oz button mushrooms,
    quartered
300 ml/½ pint chicken stock
2 cloves
1 onion, peeled
salt
freshly ground black pepper
3 Cox's Orange Pippin apples,
    peeled, cored and sliced
150 ml/¼ pint soured cream
TO GARNISH:
25 g/1 oz butter
1 Cox's Orange Pippin apple,
    cored and sliced
1 teaspoon caster sugar
sprigs of parsley

It is essential to use Cox's Orange Pippin apples in this recipe – no other apple will impart the same flavour.

1. Use the seasoned flour to coat the meat.
2. Melt the butter in a frying pan, add the meat and brown on all sides. Transfer the meat to a casserole.
3. Add the mushrooms to the frying pan and cook gently for 3 minutes. Sprinkle in any remaining seasoned flour, stir well and cook for 2 minutes. Stir in the stock and bring to the boil, stirring. Pour into the casserole.
4. Stick the cloves into the onion and push into the centre of the casserole. Season to taste with salt and pepper.

Cover and cook in a preheated oven for 1½ hours or until the pork is tender.
5. Remove the lid and stir in the apples and soured cream. Adjust the seasoning. Re-cover, return to the oven and cook for a further 15 minutes.
6. Meanwhile to prepare the garnish, melt the butter in the clean frying pan and add the apple slices. Sprinkle them with the sugar and cook on each side until glazed.
7. Pour the pork into a heated serving dish. Discard the onion and cloves. Garnish with the glazed apple slices and parsley.

PORK WITH HERB CREAM SAUCE Ⓟ

Preparation time: 15 minutes
Cooking time: H pressure 10 minutes

25 g/1 oz butter
1 small onion,
    peeled and chopped
750 g/1½ lb pork fillet, cut into
    2.5 cm/1 inch cubes
2 teaspoons chopped fresh
    parsley
2 teaspoons chopped fresh
    thyme
2 teaspoons chopped fresh sage
300 ml/½ pint chicken stock
salt
freshly ground black pepper
150 ml/¼ pint single cream

If fresh herbs are not available dried herbs can be substituted. Allow 1 teaspoon each of parsley, thyme and sage.

1. Melt the butter in the open cooker. Add the onion and fry gently until it is transparent. Add the pork and fry until it is lightly browned.
2. Add the herbs, stock and salt and pepper to taste. Stir well.
3. Close the cooker, bring to H pressure and cook for 10 minutes. Reduce the pressure quickly.
4. Stir in the cream and heat through gently. Do not boil the sauce once the cream has been added. Taste and adjust the seasoning, then serve with plain boiled rice.

Above left: Pork pippin
Centre: Pork with herb cream sauce
Above right: Apricot stuffed pork chops

APRICOT STUFFED PORK CHOPS

S

Preparation time: 15 minutes,
*   plus soaking time*
Cooking time: Low 7-9 hours
*   High 3-4 hours*

50 g/2 oz dried apricots
4 pork loin chops, cut at least
   2.5 cm/1 inch thick and
   trimmed of excess fat
50 g/2 oz butter or margarine
1 small stick celery,
   finely chopped
25 g/1 oz flaked almonds
1 teaspoon dried parsley
salt
freshly ground black pepper
150 ml/¼ pint hot beef stock
2 teaspoons cornflour
1 tablespoon cold water

1. Cover the apricots with boiling water and leave to soak for at least 8 hours.
2. Make a slit along the fat edge of each chop and carefully cut a pocket into the meat through to the bone.
3. Melt 25 g/1 oz of the butter or margarine in a frying pan. Add the celery and almonds and fry until lightly coloured. Turn into a bowl.
4. Drain the apricots and chop finely. Add to the bowl with the parsley and salt and pepper to taste. Mix thoroughly.
5. Divide the stuffing into four portions and carefully fill the pocket of each chop. Press the meat back together at the opening to hold the stuffing in place.
6. Heat the remaining butter or margarine in the frying pan. Add the

chops and brown on both sides. Transfer to the stoneware pot. Add a little salt and pepper and the hot stock.
7. Cover and cook on Low for 7-9 hours or High for 3-4 hours.
8. Thirty minutes before the cooking time is finished, lift out two of the chops. Dissolve the cornflour in the cold water and stir into the sauce until it has thickened. Taste and adjust the seasoning. Return the chops to the pot and baste with the sauce. Reheat if necessary before serving.

JUBILEE DUCKLING

Preparation time: 30 minutes
Cooking time: 1 hour
Oven: 180℃, 350°F, Gas Mark 4

25 g/1 oz butter
2 × 1.5 kg/3½ lb duckling,
    quartered
1 onion, peeled and chopped
2 tablespoons brandy
2 teaspoons lemon juice
1 × 425 g/15 oz can Morello
    cherries, drained (juice
    reserved) and stoned
1 bay leaf
150 ml/¼ pint red wine
salt
freshly ground black pepper
1 tablespoon cornflour
50 g/2 oz blanched almonds
snipped chives or chopped
    spring onions, to garnish

Black cherries can replace Morellos, but their flavour is sweeter and less distinctive.

1. Melt the butter in a frying pan, add the duckling quarters and brown on all sides. Transfer to a casserole.
2. Drain the surplus fat from the pan, leaving about 1 tablespoon. Add the onion and cook gently until softened.
3. Add the brandy and heat, then set alight and pour, flaming, over the duckling.
4. Put the lemon juice, half the reserved cherry juice, the bay leaf and red wine into the frying pan. Bring to the boil, scraping the sediment from the bottom of the pan. Season to taste with salt and pepper.
5. Pour into the casserole, then cover and cook in a preheated oven for 55 minutes or until the duckling is tender. Skim off the fat.

6. Meanwhile, dissolve the cornflour in the remaining cherry juice. Put an almond into each cherry.
7. Arrange the duckling on a heated serving dish. Keep hot. Pour the sauce into a saucepan and remove the bay leaf. Skim off the fat.
8. Stir in the dissolved cornflour and bring to the boil. Simmer until smooth and thickened. Adjust the seasoning.
9. Stir in the stuffed cherries, heat through and pour the sauce over the duckling. Garnish with chives or chopped spring onions.

DUCKLING WITH ORANGES

Preparation time: 30 minutes
Cooking time: 1 hour 10 minutes
Oven: 180℃, 350°F, Gas Mark 4

25 g/1 oz butter
2 × 1.5 kg/3½ lb duckling,
    quartered and trimmed of fat
1 onion,
    peeled and finely chopped
300 ml/½ pint giblet or chicken
    stock
2 cloves
2 oranges
juice of 1 lemon
salt
freshly ground black pepper
2 tablespoons Grand Marnier
1 teaspoon arrowroot
sprigs of parsley, to garnish

1. Melt the butter in a large frying pan, add the duckling quarters and brown well on all sides for about 10 minutes. Transfer to a casserole.
2. Pour off the surplus fat from the frying pan, leaving about 1 tablespoon. Stir in the onion and cook gently until softened. Add the stock, cloves and juice of 1 orange and the lemon and season to taste with salt and pepper.
3. Bring to the boil, then pour over the duckling. Cover the casserole and cook in a preheated oven for 1 hour, then skim off the fat.
3. Meanwhile, thinly peel the second orange (all white pith must be removed) and the rind cut into long, thin strips. Squeeze the juice and reserve.
4. Put the rind into a small saucepan, cover with cold water and bring to the boil. Simmer for 5 minutes, then drain. Stir the rind and the Grand Marnier into the casserole. Return to the oven and continue cooking for 7 minutes.
5. Arrange the duckling on a heated serving dish. Pour the sauce into a small saucepan and skim off the fat.
6. Dissolve the arrowroot in the reserved orange juice, add to the sauce and bring to the boil, stirring. Adjust the seasoning.
7. Pour the sauce over the duckling and garnish with the parsley.

Below left: Duckling with oranges
Centre: Jubilee duckling
Below right: Casserole of hare

CASSEROLE OF HARE

Preparation time: 30 minutes
Cooking time: 1½ hours
Oven: 180°C, 350°F, Gas Mark 4

3 tablespoons oil
1 small hare, jointed
2 onions, peeled and sliced
2 carrots, peeled and sliced
2 garlic cloves,
    peeled and crushed
450 ml/¾ pint stock
150 ml/¼ pint port
juice of 1 lemon
1 bouquet garni
salt
freshly ground black pepper

TOPPING:
25 g/1 oz butter
100 g/4 oz streaky bacon, in the
    piece, rind removed, cubed
100 g/4 oz button mushrooms
chopped fresh parsley

25 g/1 oz butter
25 g/1 oz plain flour

The blood of the hare is traditionally used to thicken this stew, but is seldom available now.

1. Heat the oil in a large frying pan, add the hare joints and brown on all sides. Transfer to a casserole.
2. Stir the onions and carrots into the oil in the frying pan and cook gently until the onions begin to turn golden brown. Pour off the surplus oil.
3. Add the garlic, stock, port, lemon juice and bouquet garni. Season to taste with salt and plenty of black pepper.
4. Bring to the boil, then pour over the hare in the casserole. Tuck a piece of greaseproof paper over the stew. Cover the casserole and cook in a preheated oven for 1¼ hours or until the hare is very tender.
5. Meanwhile, melt the butter for the topping in a frying pan, add the bacon cubes and cook gently for 5 minutes. Remove from the pan. Add the

mushrooms to the pan and cook for 5 minutes. Drain and keep hot on separate plates.
6. Arrange the hare in a heated serving dish and keep hot.
7. Strain the sauce into a saucepan and bring slowly to the boil.
8. Mix the butter and flour into a paste and whisk into the sauce in small pieces. Simmer, stirring, until it thickens. Adjust the seasoning.
9. Pour the sauce over the hare, and top with the bacon, mushrooms and parsley.

BRAISED VENISON WITH MORELLO CHERRIES

*Preparation time: 1½ hours,
plus marinating time*
Cooking time: 2½ hours
Oven: 160℃, 325°F, Gas Mark 3

175 ml/6 fl oz red wine
1 onion, peeled and sliced
1 tablespoon brandy
2 tablespoons oil
sprig of fresh thyme, or
    ½ teaspoon dried thyme
parsley stalks
1 bay leaf
1 kg/2 lb boned venison
    shoulder, cut into 4 cm/1½
    inch cubes
25 g/1 oz butter
1 tablespoon oil
100 g/4 oz streaky bacon in the
    piece, rind removed, diced
2 medium onions,
    peeled and finely chopped
2 tablespoons plain flour
1 × 425 g/15 oz can Morello
    cherries, drained (juice
    reserved) and stoned
about 300 ml/½ pint venison or
    beef stock
2 garlic cloves,
    peeled and crushed
sprig of fresh rosemary or pinch
    of dried rosemary
1 bay leaf
salt
freshly ground black pepper
TARTLETS:
8 small shortcrust pastry tartlet
    cases, baked blind
1 tablespoon redcurrant jelly
pinch of ground cinnamon
spray of fresh rosemary, or
    chopped fresh parsley,
    to garnish

1. In a large bowl mix together the red wine, 1 sliced onion, brandy, oil, thyme, parsley stalks and bay leaf for the marinade.
2. Add the venison, cover and leave in a cool place for 24 hours, turning the meat over several times.
3. When ready, lift out the meat; strain the marinade and reserve it.
4. Melt the butter with the oil in a flameproof casserole, add the bacon and cook for 5 minutes. Add the onions and fry gently until softened.
5. Stir in the flour and cook for 2-3 minutes, then stir in the reserved marinade, the cherry juice and 300 ml/½ pint stock. Bring slowly to the boil, stirring.
6. Remove from the heat and add the venison, garlic, rosemary and bay leaf. If the liquid does not come to the level of the meat, add a little more stock. Season to taste with salt and pepper.
7. Cover and cook in a preheated oven for 2 hours. Remove the lid, baste with the sauce and return to the oven, uncovered. Cook for a further 30 minutes, basting from time to time.
8. Heat the tartlet cases in the oven.
9. Put the cherries, redcurrant jelly and cinnamon in a small saucepan and heat gently. Fill the tartlet cases with the cherry mixture.
10. Turn the venison and sauce into a heated serving dish. Adjust the seasoning and discard the rosemary sprig and bay leaf. Garnish with fresh rosemary or sprinkle with parsley, and serve with the cherry tartlets.

**Right: Braised venison
with morello cherries**

BEEF MARINATED IN WINE

Preparation time: 15 minutes,
plus marinating time
Cooking time: H pressure 20 minutes

750 g/1½ lb chuck steak,
   trimmed of excess fat and cut
   into 2.5 cm/1 inch cubes
1 large onion, peeled and sliced
1 garlic clove, peeled and
   crushed
½ teaspoon dried thyme
2 tablespoons olive oil
300 ml/½ pint red wine
50 g/2 oz butter
1 tablespoon tomato purée
150 ml/¼ pint brown stock
salt
freshly ground black pepper
1 tablespoon plain flour

1. Place the meat cubes in a mixing bowl and add the onion, garlic, thyme, olive oil and 150 ml/¼ pint of the wine. Stir well, then leave to marinate, covered, for several hours or overnight in the refrigerator.
2. Melt 25 g/1 oz of the butter in the open cooker. Drain the meat and vegetables well, reserving the liquid, and add them to the cooker. Fry until the meat is lightly browned.
3. Add the reserved marinade liquid to the cooker together with the remaining 150 ml/¼ pint wine, the tomato purée, stock and salt and pepper to taste. Stir well.
4. Close the cooker, bring to H pressure and cook for 20 minutes. Reduce the pressure quickly.

5. Return the open cooker to the heat. Mix the remaining butter with the flour to make a paste and add to the sauce in small pieces. Simmer, stirring, until the sauce thickens.
6. Taste and adjust the seasoning before serving with buttered noodles.

Below left: Beef marinated in wine
Below right: Beef with Madeira
and mushroom sauce

BEEF WITH MADEIRA & MUSHROOM SAUCE

Preparation time: 7 minutes,
plus marinating time
Cooking time: H pressure 30 minutes

40 g/1½ oz butter
1 kg/2 lb piece of topside of beef
1 medium onion,
   peeled and chopped
175 g/6 oz button mushrooms,
   sliced
300 ml/½ pint Madeira
150 ml/¼ pint water
salt
freshly ground black pepper
2 teaspoons plain flour
few fresh parsley sprigs.

1. Melt 25 g/1 oz of the butter in the open cooker, add the beef and brown well on all sides. Lift it out, draining well.
2. Add the onion and 100 g/4 oz of the mushrooms to the cooker and fry gently until the onion is lightly browned.
3. Return the meat to the cooker. Add the Madeira, water, and salt and pepper to taste.
4. Close the cooker, bring to H pressure and cook for 30 minutes. Reduce the pressure quickly.
5. Lift out the beef, remove any strings and keep hot.
6. Return the open cooker to the heat. Mix the remaining butter with the flour to

make a paste and add to the sauce in small pieces. Simmer, stirring, until the sauce thickens. Add the remaining mushrooms, taste and adjust the seasoning and continue to simmer for 2 minutes.
7. Slice the beef thickly and arrange on a heated serving dish. Pour over the mushroom sauce and garnish with small sprigs of parsley.

MOULDED SPICED BEEF

Preparation time: 15 minutes
Cooking time: 3¼ hours
Oven: 160°C, 325°F, Gas Mark 3

1 kg/2 lb thick flank of beef
1 veal knuckle, cracked
1 onion, peeled and stuck with
    4 cloves
1 carrot,
    trimmed and lightly scraped
1 stick celery, cut into 3
1 bay leaf
½ teaspoon blade mace
½ teaspoon dry mustard
½ teaspoon whole allspice
    berries
1 teaspoon black peppercorns
1 tablespoon wine vinegar
900 ml/1½ pints beef stock
½ teaspoon salt
TO GARNISH:
tomato wedges
sprigs of watercress

1. Place all the ingredients in a large casserole, cover and cook in a preheated oven for 1½ hours.
2. Skim, then continue cooking for a further 1½ hours or until the meat is very tender.
3. Lift the meat on to a dish and allow to cool a little. Strain the broth and leave to cool.
4. Remove the bone and gristle from the knuckle, and cut the veal and beef in 1 cm/½ inch dice.
5. Skim the fat from the broth, then stir in the meat. Adjust the seasoning. Chill until beginning to thicken.
6. Stir to distribute the meat evenly and turn into a dampened mould. Chill until set.
7. Turn out on to a serving dish, garnish with tomato wedges and watercress, and serve with potato salad.

TONGUE WITH MADEIRA

Preparation time: 30 minutes,
    plus soaking time
Cooking time: about 3½ hours
Oven: 160°C, 325°F, Gas Mark 3

1 × 1¼ kg/2½-2¾ lb ox tongue,
    soaked in several changes of
    cold water for at least 2-3
    hours
3 onions, peeled
3 carrots, trimmed and scraped
2 cloves
bunch of parsley
50 g/2 oz butter
3 tomatoes,
    skinned, seeded and sliced
1 garlic clove,
    peeled and crushed
50 g/2 oz seedless raisins
50 g/2 oz walnuts,
    coarsely chopped
300 ml/½ pint strong beef stock
    or canned consommé
150 ml/¼ pint Madeira
salt
freshly ground black pepper
3 tablespoons double cream
    (optional)
TO GARNISH:
orange segments,
    free of pith and skin
sprigs of watercress

Beef stock or consommé is preferable to using the liquid the tongue has been cooked in. This can be used in a soup.

1. Place the drained tongue in a flameproof casserole with 1 whole onion, 1 carrot, the cloves and parsley. Cover with cold water and bring very slowly to the boil.
2. Cover and simmer for 2½ hours or until tender when pierced with a skewer.
3. Allow to cool for about 1 hour in the liquid, then drain the tongue.
4. Remove the skin and gristle and the small bones at the thick end of the tongue. Cut the tongue into slices.
5. Finely chop the remaining onions and carrots.
6. Melt the butter in the rinsed casserole, add the chopped vegetables and fry until the onions are softened.
7. Add the tomatoes, garlic, raisins, walnuts, stock or consommé, Madeira and salt and pepper to taste. Mix well, bring to the boil and remove from the heat.
8. Add the tongue slices to the sauce. Cover the casserole and cook in a preheated oven for 45 minutes.
9. Adjust the seasoning. Pour the cream, if using, over the tongue. Do not mix.
10. Garnish with orange segments and watercress, and serve with creamed potato, well flavoured with nutmeg.

BEEF, SAGE & HAM ROULADES [S]

Preparation time: 25 minutes
Cooking time: Low 8-10 hours
High 4-5 hours

8 thin slices of topside of beef,
   beaten
8 slices of cooked shoulder ham
50 g/2 oz fresh white
   breadcrumbs
50 g/2 oz mushrooms, chopped
1 teaspoon dried sage
1 garlic clove, peeled and
   crushed
salt
freshly ground black pepper
1 egg, beaten
50 g/2 oz butter
1 × 225 g/8 oz can tomatoes,
   chopped, with their juice
150 ml/¼ pint red wine
TO FINISH:
1 dessertspoon cornflour
1 tablespoon cold water
fresh sage leaves

1. Lay the slices of beef on a board and cover each one with a slice of ham.
2. Mix together the breadcrumbs, mushrooms, sage, garlic and salt and pepper to taste. Add sufficient egg to bind the ingredients together.
3. Divide the stuffing between the slices of beef. Spread it almost to the edges. Roll up tightly and secure the roulades with pieces of fine string at each end.
4. Melt the butter in a frying pan. Add the roulades and brown on all sides. Transfer to the stoneware pot.
5. Add the tomatoes and wine to the pan and stir well. Heat thoroughly, then pour over the roulades.
6. Cover and cook on Low for 8-10 hours or High for 4-5 hours.
7. Lift out the roulades and remove the strings. Dissolve the cornflour in the cold water and stir into the sauce until it has thickened. Return the roulades to the sauce and reheat if necessary. Taste and adjust the seasoning. Garnish with sage leaves before serving.

GINGERED BEEF PATTIES

Preparation time: 30 minutes
Cooking time: 50 minutes
Oven: 180°C, 350°F, Gas Mark 4

450 g/1 lb minced beef
1 onion,
   peeled and very finely
   chopped
50 g/2 oz fresh brown or white
   breadcrumbs
1 egg, beaten
2 tablespoons chopped fresh
   parsley
salt
freshly ground black pepper
2 tablespoons oil
300 ml/½ pint beef stock
1 tablespoon dark brown sugar
1 teaspoon ground ginger
50 g/2 oz seedless raisins
juice of 1 lemon
25 g/1 oz butter
8 pineapple slices,
   fresh or canned
2 teaspoons arrowroot
TO GARNISH:
lemon twists
preserved ginger, sliced

This recipe is at its best made with fresh pineapple.

1. Mix together the beef, onion, breadcrumbs, egg and parsley, working well with a wet hand. Season thoroughly with salt and pepper. Shape into 8 patties.
2. Heat the oil in a large frying pan, add the patties and brown well on both sides. Transfer to a flameproof casserole.
3. Mix together the stock, sugar, ginger, raisins and lemon juice and pour over the patties. Cover the casserole and cook in a preheated oven for 45 minutes.
4. Meanwhile, melt the butter in the frying pan, add the pineapple slices and brown lightly on each side. Transfer to a heated serving dish.
5. Lift the patties from the casserole and place one on each pineapple slice.
6. Dissolve the arrowroot in a little cold water and stir into the sauce. Bring to the boil, stirring. Adjust the seasoning, then pour the sauce over the patties. Garnish with lemon twists and ginger.

Top left: Moulded spiced beef
Top right: Beef, sage and ham roulades
Bottom left: Tongue with Madeira
Bottom right: Gingered beef patties

LAMB & LEMON CASSEROLE

Preparation time: 25 minutes
Cooking time: 1¼ hours
Oven: 160°C, 325°F, Gas Mark 3

1½ tablespoons oil
750 g/1¼ lb lamb fillet, cut into
    5 cm/2 inch pieces
1 onion, peeled and sliced
50 g/2 oz cooked ham, diced
2 teaspoons chopped fresh
    parsley
2 teaspoons chopped fresh
    marjoram
300 ml/¼ pint dry white wine
salt
freshly ground black pepper
grated rind and juice of 1 lemon
3 egg yolks, beaten
cooked green asparagus spears,
    to garnish

1. Heat the oil in a flameproof casserole, add the lamb and brown well. Add the onion and cook gently for 5 minutes.
2. Stir in the ham, herbs and wine, and season to taste with salt and pepper. Cover and cook in a preheated oven for 1 hour or until the lamb is tender.
3. Mix the lemon rind and juice into the casserole. Stir a ladleful of the hot liquid into the egg yolks, then pour back into the pot. Heat gently on top of the stove, stirring, until the sauce thickens. Do not boil. Adjust the seasoning.
4. Pour into a heated serving dish and garnish with asparagus spears.

Top right: Tajine of lamb
Centre: Lamb and lemon casserole
Bottom right: Lamb romana

KIDNEYS NAPOLEON   S

Preparation time: 20 minutes
Cooking time: Low 6-8 hours
    High 3-4 hours

225 g/8 oz thick gammon rasher,
    trimmed of fat
25 g/1 oz butter
1 medium onion,
    peeled and chopped
750 g/1¼ lb lambs' kidneys,
    skinned, halved lengthways
    and cored
4-6 tablespoons brandy
300 ml/½ pint hot beef stock
1 bay leaf
salt
freshly ground black pepper
2 teaspoons cornflour
chopped fresh parsley,
    to garnish

This is a deliciously rich and strong-flavoured dish.

1. Cut the gammon into thin strips, about 5 × 1 cm/2 × ½ inch.
2. Melt the butter in a frying pan, add the onion and fry until lightly browned. Transfer to the stoneware pot.
3. Add the kidneys and gammon to the pan and fry briskly until they are browned on all sides. Carefully drain off any excess fat or liquid from the pan.
4. Warm 2-4 tablespoons of the brandy in a small saucepan and pour over the kidneys and gammon. Set alight and leave until the flames die down.
5. Transfer the meat to the stoneware pot and add the stock, bay leaf and salt and pepper to taste.
6. Cover and cook on Low for 6-8 hours or High for 3-4 hours.
7. Dissolve the cornflour in the remaining brandy. Stir into the sauce until it has thickened. Discard the bay leaf. Taste and adjust the seasoning.
8. Sprinkle with parsley before serving.

Right: Kidneys Napoleon

TAJINE OF LAMB

Preparation time: 10 minutes, plus
*   soaking time*
Cooking time: 2-2½ hours
Oven: 160°C, 325°F, Gas Mark 3

750 g/1½ lb boned leg of lamb,
    cubed
2 medium onions,
    peeled and finely chopped
2 tablespoons olive oil
½ teaspoon ground coriander
½ teaspoon ground ginger
1 teaspoon ground cinnamon
225 g/8 oz dried pears,
    soaked in water overnight
    and drained
2 tablespoons clear honey
600 ml/1 pint chicken stock
salt
freshly ground black pepper
1 tablespoon cornflour
2 teaspoons orange flower
    water
TO GARNISH:
spray fresh coriander leaves
toasted pine nuts

Orange flower water and fresh coriander
are available at Indian shops, and dried
pears and pine nuts are available from
health food shops and some
supermarkets.

1. Put the lamb, onion, olive oil, spices,
pears, honey and stock into a casserole.
Season to taste with salt and pepper.
2. Cover and cook in a preheated oven
for 2 hours. If the meat is not tender after
this time, return it to the oven for a
further 25 minutes.
3. Arrange the lamb and pears on a
heated serving dish and keep hot. Pour
the sauce into a small saucepan.
4. Dissolve the cornflour in a little cold
water, stir into the sauce and bring to the
boil, stirring. Adjust the seasoning.
5. Pour the sauce over the lamb, sprinkle
the surface with the orange flower water
and garnish with coriander leaves and
toasted pine nuts.

LAMB ROMANA $\boxed{\text{S}}$

Preparation time: 20 minutes,
*   plus marinating time*
Cooking time: Low 8-10 hours
*   High 4-5 hours*

750 g/1½ lb boned leg of lamb,
    trimmed of excess fat and cut
    into 2.5 cm/1 inch cubes
1 garlic clove, peeled and
    crushed
175 g/6 oz small onions, peeled
1 small green pepper,
    cored, seeded and sliced
1 teaspoon dried basil
1 teaspoon dried marjoram
2 tablespoons olive oil
300 ml/½ pint red Italian wine
50 g/2 oz butter
100 g/4 oz button mushrooms
salt
freshly ground black pepper
1 tablespoon plain flour
few fresh parsley sprigs,
    to garnish

1. Place the lamb cubes in a large bowl
with the garlic, onions, green pepper,
herbs, oil and 150 ml/¼ pint of the wine.
Cover and leave to marinate in the
refrigerator for at least 4 hours.
2. Drain off the marinade liquid and
reserve. Melt 25 g/1 oz of the butter in a
frying pan. Add the meat and vegetables
and fry briskly for 2-3 minutes. Transfer
to the stoneware pot, draining well.
3. Add the mushrooms, reserved
marinade liquid and remaining wine to
the pan and bring to the boil, stirring
well. Pour over the meat in the stoneware
pot and season to taste with salt and
pepper.
4. Cover and cook on Low for 8-10 hours
or High for 4-5 hours.
5. Thirty minutes before the cooking time
is finished, mix the remaining butter with
the flour to make a paste. Add to the
sauce in small pieces and stir until the
sauce thickens. Taste and adjust the
seasoning.
6. Serve on a bed of buttered noodles or
rice, garnished with small sprigs of
parsley.

VEAU VERONIQUE

Preparation time: 40 minutes
Cooking time: 1 hour
Oven: 180°C, 350°F, Gas Mark 4

25 g/1 oz butter
1 tablespoon oil
75 g/3 oz shallots,
    peeled and finely chopped
750 g/1½ lb veal fillet, cut into
    5 cm/2 inch pieces
150 ml/¼ pint dry white wine
150 ml/¼ pint strong veal or
    chicken stock
pinch of cayenne
salt
freshly ground black pepper
1 teaspoon chopped fresh
    marjoram, or ½ teaspoon
    dried marjoram
225 g/8 oz white grapes,
    peeled and pipped
4 tablespoons soured cream
2 teaspoons lemon juice
15 g/½ oz plain flour and 15 g/
    ½ oz butter (optional)
TO GARNISH:
toasted flaked almonds
few clusters of black grapes,
    pipped

1. Melt the butter with the oil in a flameproof casserole. Add the shallots and fry until softened.
2. Add the veal and turn over in the butter to stiffen, not colour.
3. Stir in the white wine, stock, cayenne, salt and pepper to taste, the marjoram and grapes. Cover and cook in a preheated oven for 55 minutes or until the veal is tender.
4. Stir in the cream and lemon juice.

5. If a thick sauce is preferred, mix the flour with the 15 g/½ oz butter to make a paste and whisk this into the sauce in small pieces. Bring to the boil, stirring. Adjust the seasoning.
6. Serve from the casserole or poured into a heated serving dish, garnished with almonds and black grapes.

VARIATION:
Use pork fillet instead of the veal.

VEAL IN VERMOUTH [S]

Preparation time: 15 minutes
Cooking time: Low 7-9 hours
    High 3-4 hours

75 g/3 oz butter
750 g-1 kg/1½-2 lb pie veal,
    trimmed of excess fat and cut
    into 2.5 cm/1 inch cubes
1 small onion,
    peeled and chopped
100 g/4 oz mushrooms, sliced
300 ml/½ pint dry vermouth
salt
freshly ground black pepper
1 tablespoon plain flour
4 mushrooms, sliced, to garnish

1. Melt 50 g/2 oz of the butter in a frying pan. Add the veal and onion and fry until the veal is lightly browned. Transfer to the stoneware pot, draining well.
2. Add the mushrooms and vermouth to the pan and bring to the boil, stirring well. Pour over the meat in the stoneware pot and season to taste with a little salt and pepper.
3. Cover and cook on Low for 7-9 hours or High for 3-4 hours.
4. Thirty minutes before the cooking time is finished, mix the remaining butter with the flour to make a paste. Add to the sauce in small pieces and stir until the sauce begins to thicken. Taste and adjust the seasoning.
5. Garnish with the raw sliced mushrooms.

VEAL TOKANY

Preparation time: 30 minutes
Cooking time: 1½ hours
Oven: 160°C, 325°F, Gas Mark 3

50 g/2 oz seasoned flour
750 g/1½ lb boned veal
  shoulder, cut into 5 cm/2 inch
  pieces
25 g/1 oz butter
2 tablespoons oil
2 onions, peeled and sliced
1-2 red peppers, cored, seeded
  and cut into thin rings
2 garlic cloves,
  peeled and crushed
1 teaspoon chopped fresh dill or
  ½ teaspoon dried dill
1 tablespoon sweet Hungarian
  paprika
150 ml/¼ pint dry white wine
150 ml/¼ pint veal of beef stock
salt
freshly ground black pepper
75 g/3 oz streaky bacon,
  rind removed, diced
100 g/4 oz button mushrooms,
  quartered
150 ml/¼ pint soured cream
fronds of fresh dill, to garnish

1. Use the seasoned flour to coat the veal.
2. Melt the butter with the oil in a flameproof casserole, add the veal and brown on all sides. Remove the veal and reserve.
3. Add the onions to the pot and cook gently until softened. Add the pepper rings and continue cooking for 5 minutes, then stir in the garlic, dill, paprika and any remaining seasoned flour. Cook for 3 minutes.
4. Stir in the wine and stock, and season to taste with salt and pepper. Bring to the boil, stirring, then return the veal to the casserole.
5. Cover and cook in a preheated oven for 1¼ hours or until the veal is tender.
6. Meanwhile, put the bacon into a saucepan, cover with cold water and bring to the boil. Drain and refresh under cold water. Pat dry with kitchen paper.
7. Fry the bacon in a frying pan until the fat runs. Drain and add to the casserole with the mushrooms and soured cream. Mix well. Adjust the seasoning. Re-cover and cook for a further 15 minutes.
8. Pour into a heated serving dish and garnish with dill. Serve with buttered noodles and a green salad.

BRAISED VEAL WITH FENNEL

Preparation time: 20 minutes
Cooking time: 1¼ hours
Oven: 160°C, 325°F, Gas Mark 3

50 g/2 oz butter
1 tablespoon oil
2 medium onions,
  peeled and thinly sliced
40 g/1½ oz seasoned flour
750 g/1½ lb boned veal shoulder,
  cut into 5 cm/2 inch pieces
300 ml/½ pint veal or chicken
  stock
1 garlic clove,
  peeled and crushed
2 fennel bulbs, thinly sliced
salt
freshly ground black pepper
4 tomatoes,
  skinned and quartered
fronds of fennel, to garnish

1. Melt the butter and oil in a flameproof casserole, add the onions and cook gently until golden brown. Lift on to a plate.
2. Use the seasoned flour to coat the veal. Add the veal to the casserole and brown the pieces on all sides.
3. Stir in any remaining seasoned flour and cook for 2 minutes. Return the onions to the casserole, stir in the stock and bring to the boil.
4. Remove from the heat, add the garlic and fennel and season to taste with salt and pepper. Cover and cook in a preheated oven for 1 hour or until the veal is tender.
5. Add the tomatoes to the casserole, re-cover and cook for a further 15 minutes. Adjust the seasoning.
6. Turn into a heated serving dish and garnish with fronds of fennel.
Serve with buttered new potatoes and a green salad.

Below left: Veau Veronique
Centre: Veal tokany
Below right: Braised veal with fennel

Left: Veal in vermouth

CASSEROLE OF SCALLOPS WITH CREAM

Preparation time: 20 minutes
Cooking time: 30 minutes
Oven: 160°C, 325°F, Gas Mark 3

8 large scallops, fresh, or frozen
    and thawed
50 g/2 oz butter
25 g/1 oz shallots,
    peeled and sliced
225 g/8 oz mushrooms, sliced
2 garlic cloves,
    peeled and crushed
2 teaspoons tomato purée
4-6 tablespoons sherry
salt
freshly ground black pepper
250 ml/8 fl oz double cream
2 egg yolks, beaten
2 teaspoons lemon juice
2 tablespoons chopped fresh
    parsley

1. Detach the coral from the scallops, and slice each scallop in half into two rounds.
2. Melt the butter in a flameproof casserole, add the scallops and coral and cook very gently for 5 minutes. Lift them on to a plate.
3. Add the shallots, mushrooms and garlic to the pot and cook gently for 2 minutes, turning the vegetables over in the butter.
4. Mix the tomato purée into the sherry and stir into the vegetables. Heat gently, then remove from the stove.
5. Replace the scallops and coral in the casserole and season to taste with salt and pepper. Cover and cook in a preheated

oven for 20 minutes.
6. Transfer the scallops, coral and vegetables to a heated serving dish and keep hot. Stir the cream and egg yolks together and add to the casserole, together with the scallops. Stirring constantly over gentle heat, cook until the sauce thickens. Do not let it boil.
7. Stir in the lemon juice and 1 tablespoon parsley. Adjust the seasoning. Pour the sauce over the scallops, and garnish with the remaining parsley. Serve with Mange tout and new potatoes or braised rice with almonds.

MOULES MARINIÈRE

Serves 4-6
Preparation time: 30 minutes
Cooking time: H pressure 1 minute

1½ kg/3 lb fresh mussels
1 medium onion,
    peeled and finely chopped
2 garlic cloves,
    peeled and crushed
2 fresh thyme·sprigs
2 parsley stalks
300 ml/½ pint dry white wine
freshly ground black pepper
2 tablespoons chopped fresh
    parsley, to finish

1. Discard any mussels which are already open or have broken shells. Wash and scrub the mussels under cold running water. Remove any beards from the edge of the sheels.
2. Put the mussels in the cooker with the onion, garlic, herbs, wine and pepper to taste.
3. Close the cooker, bring to H pressure and cook for 1 minute. Reduce the pressure quickly.
4. Transfer the mussels to a large heated serving dish, removing the top half of the shells. Discard any mussels that have not opened.

5. Return the open cooker to the heat. Remove the herb stalks and boil the liquid briskly for 2 minutes. Taste and adjust the seasoning. Add the chopped parsley and pour over the mussels. Serve immediately.

SOLE & PRAWN PAUPIETTES [P]

Preparation time: 10 minutes
Cooking time: H pressure 3 minutes

8 lemon sole fillets, skinned
2 tablespoons lemon juice
175 g/6 oz cooked shelled
  prawns
freshly ground black pepper
150 ml/¼ pint milk
150 ml/¼ pint water
1 bay leaf
2 small fresh parsley sprigs
SAUCE:
25 g/1 oz butter or margarine
25 g/1 oz plain flour
about 150 ml/¼ pint milk
2 teaspoons anchovy essence

1. Lay the sole fillets, skinned side up, on a board. Sprinkle each with a little of the lemon juice.
2. Set aside 8 of the prawns for the garnish and chop the remainder. Put a little of the chopped prawns on each sole fillet with some pepper. Roll up tightly from the tail end and secure with a wooden cocktail stick.
3. Put the milk and water in the cooker and add the bay leaf and parsley. Grease the trivet and put it in the cooker. Place the rolled fillets on the trivet.
4. Close the cooker, bring to H pressure and cook for 3 minutes. Reduce the pressure quickly.

5. Lift out the fish and remove the cocktail sticks. Keep hot on a heated serving dish.
6. Strain the liquid, discarding the bay leaf and parsley, and reserve. Rinse and dry the cooker.
7. Melt the butter or margarine in the open cooker. Stir in the flour and cook for 1-2 minutes. Remove from the heat and stir in the milk and the reserved liquid. Return to the heat and bring to the boil, stirring. Stir in the anchovy essence and simmer for 1 minute. Taste and adjust the seasoning. Pour the sauce around the sole.
8. Garnish each paupiette with a reserved prawn before serving.

TROUT IN WHITE WINE [S]

Preparation time: 10 minutes
Cooking time: Low 4-5 hours
*   High 2-2½ hours*

4 trout, cleaned
100 g/4 oz mushrooms, sliced
¼ teaspoon dried dill
salt
freshly ground black pepper
150 ml/¼ pint dry white wine

1. Lay the prepared trout in the stoneware pot.
2. Cover with the mushrooms and sprinkle over the dill and salt and pepper to taste. Pour over the wine.
3. Cover and cook on Low for 4-5 hours or High for 2-2½ hours. Serve hot, or leave to cool in the cooking liquid and serve cold with salad.

Far left: Casseroles of scallops with cream
Centre left: Moules marinière
Centre right: Sole and prawn paupiettes
Far right: Trout in white wine

MEALS-IN-A-POT

NEW ENGLAND BEEF DINNER

Preparation time: 20 minutes
Cooking time: 3½-4 hours

1 × 1½ kg/3 lb joint salt brisket
  of beef
1 bay leaf, parsley stalks, sprig
  of fresh thyme (or 1 bouquet
  garni)
1 teaspoon black peppercorns
4 cloves
1 onion, peeled
8 carrots,
  scraped and halved
  lengthways
8 small potatoes,
  peeled and halved
1 small tight cabbage,
  quartered and cored
chopped fresh parsley, to
  garnish

1. Put the brisket into a deep flameproof casserole, cover with cold water and add the herbs or bouquet garni and peppercorns.
2. Stick the cloves into the onion and add to the pot. Cover and bring very slowly to the boil, skimming off the scum.
3. Cover and simmer very gently for 3 hours.
4. Add the carrots and potatoes, re-cover and continue simmering for 20 minutes.
5. Stir in the cabbage, re-cover and cook for a further 20-30 minutes or until the meat and vegetables are tender.
6. Remove the meat to a board, slice it and arrange the slices in a heated serving dish. Surround with the drained carrots, potatoes and cabbage.
7. Strain the broth, adjust the seasoning and pour a little over the meat; serve the remainder separately.
8. Sprinkle with chopped parsley. Serve with plenty of fresh crusty bread to mop up the broth.

COUNTRY BEEF & HERBY BREAD   S

Preparation time: 15 minutes
Cooking time: Low 8-10 hours
   High 4-5 hours

2 tablespoons oil
1 large onion,
   peeled and chopped
3 medium carrots,
   scraped and sliced
3 celery sticks, chopped
750 g/1½ lb stewing beef,
   trimmed of excess fat and cut
   into 2.5 cm/1 inch cubes
1 × 400 g/14 oz can tomatoes,
   chopped, with their juice
150 ml/¼ pint beef stock
salt
freshly ground black pepper
1 bouquet garni
TOPPING:
40 g/1½ oz butter
1 teaspoon dried mixed herbs
6 thick slices of French bread

1. Heat the oil in a frying pan. Add the onion, carrots and celery and fry until they are lightly browned. Transfer to the stoneware pot, draining well.
2. Add the beef to the frying pan and brown on all sides. Transfer to the stoneware pot.
3. Add the tomatoes, stock and salt and pepper to taste to the frying pan and bring to the boil. Pour into the stoneware pot and add the bouquet garni.
4. Cover and cook on Low for 8-10 hours or High for 4-5 hours.
5. To make the topping, cream together the butter and herbs and spread on one side of each piece of bread.
6. Thirty minutes before the cooking time is completed, remove the bouquet garni. Taste and adjust the seasoning. Press the bread, buttered side up, into the liquid. (If your slow cooker has a removable stoneware pot the bread can be crisped before serving by placing under a hot grill for a few minutes.)

MINCED BEEF NAPOLI   S

Preparation time: 5 minutes
Cooking time: Low 6 hours
   High 3 hours

1 tablespoon oil
750 g/1½ lb minced beef
1 medium onion,
   peeled and chopped
50 g/2 oz mushrooms, chopped
1 × 400 g/14 oz can tomatoes,
   chopped, with their juice
1 teaspoon dried oregano
150 ml/¼ pint hot beef stock
salt
freshly ground black pepper
100 g/4 oz pasta shells

1. Heat the oil in a frying pan, add the beef and onion and brown quickly. Transfer to the stoneware pot and stir in the mushrooms, tomatoes, oregano, stock and salt and pepper to taste.
2. Cover and cook on Low for 4 hours or High for 2 hours.
3. Add the pasta and stir well. Cover again and continue cooking for 2 hours on Low or 1 hour on High.
4. Taste and adjust the seasoning.

Right: Minced beef Napoli
Far right: Spiced braised beef
with vegetables

HUNGARIAN MEATBALL & POTATO CASSEROLE P

Preparation time: 25 minutes
Cooking time: H pressure 4 minutes

750 g/1½ lb minced beef
50 g/2 oz fresh white
  breadcrumbs
1 small onion, peeled and
  grated
2 teaspoons paprika
½ teaspoon grated nutmeg
salt
freshly ground black pepper
1 egg, beaten
2 tablespoons oil
1 × 400 g/14 oz can tomatoes,
  chopped, with their juice
300 ml/½ pint beef stock
450 g/1 lb potatoes, peeled and
  cut into 25 g/1 oz pieces

In the summer, new potatoes are ideal for this recipe; in the winter use a variety that is not too floury when cooked.

1. Mix together the minced beef, breadcrumbs, onion, paprika, nutmeg and salt and pepper to taste. Bind with the beaten egg.
2. Turn out on to a well-floured surface and divide the beef mixture into 18 pieces. Shape into balls.
3. Heat the oil in the open cooker. Add the meatballs, a few at a time, and brown on all sides.
4. Drain off any excess fat from the cooker, then return all the meatballs to it. Add the tomatoes, stock, potatoes and a little salt and pepper. Stir well.
5. Close the cooker, bring to H pressure and cook for 4 minutes. Reduce the pressure quickly.
6. Taste and adjust the seasoning before serving.

Far left: Country beef and herby bread
Left: Hungarian meatball and potato casserole

SPICED BRAISED BEEF WITH VEGETABLES P

Preparation time: 10 minutes
Cooking time: H pressure 15 minutes

2 tablespoons oil
1 small onion, peeled and sliced
750 g/1½ lb braising steak,
  sliced 2 cm/¾ inch thick and
  cut into 4 portions
50 g/2 oz mushrooms, sliced
1 × 400 g/14 oz can tomatoes,
  chopped, with their juice
4 tablespoons water
1 tablespoon demerara sugar
1 teaspoon dry mustard
½ teaspoon ground allspice
salt
freshly ground black pepper
450 g/1 lb potatoes, peeled and
  cut into 25 g/1 oz pieces
350 g/12 oz frozen peas or
  green beans
1 dessertspoon cornflour
1 tablespoon water

1. Heat the oil in the open cooker. Add the onion and fry until lightly browned. Add the braising steak and brown on both sides. Lift out the steak and onions, draining off any excess fat.
2. Add the mushrooms, tomatoes, water, sugar, mustard, allspice and salt and pepper to taste to the cooker. Stir well, then lay the pieces of steak and the onions on top.
3. Close the cooker, bring to H pressure and cook for 11 minutes. Reduce the pressure quickly.
4. Place the trivet over the meat and pile the potatoes on top. Sprinkle with a little salt. Put the open cooker back on the heat. When the liquid is boiling again, add the separator containing the salted peas or beans.
5. Close the cooker again, bring to H pressure and cook for 4 minutes. Reduce the pressure quickly.
6. Lift out the vegetables and meat and keep them hot. Blend the cornflour with the water, stir into the sauce and bring to the boil. Serve separately.

LAMB CASSEROLE

Preparation time: 40 minutes
Cooking time: 1 hour
Oven: 180°C, 350°F, Gas Mark 4

100 g/4 oz butter
1 onion,
    peeled and finely chopped
1 garlic clove,
    peeled and crushed
450 g/1 lb cooked lamb, minced
300 ml/½ pint lamb or chicken
    stock
½ teaspoon dried or finely
    chopped fresh rosemary
225 g/8 oz shelled peas
salt
freshly ground black pepper
1 kg/2 lb potatoes, peeled
300 ml/½ pint milk
15 g/½ oz plain flour
50 g/2 oz mature Cheddar
    cheese, grated
½ teaspoon made mustard
4 tomatoes,
    skinned, seeded and diced
sprig of fresh rosemary,
    to garnish

1. Melt 50 g/2 oz of the butter in a flameproof casserole, add the onion and cook gently until soft and golden.
2. Stir in the garlic, lamb, stock, rosemary and peas and season to taste with salt and pepper.
3. Bring to the boil, then cover and transfer to a preheated oven. Cook for 40 minutes.
4. Meanwhile, cook the potatoes in boiling water until tender. Drain well, then mash with 4 tablespoons of the milk and 25 g/1 oz of the remaining butter.
5. Melt the remaining 25 g/1 oz of the butter in a saucepan, stir in the flour and cook for 2-3 minutes.
6. Gradually stir in the remaining 150 ml/¼ pint milk, bring to the boil and simmer for 5 minutes. Stir in 40 g/1½ oz of the cheese and the mustard. Season to taste with salt and pepper. Add the tomatoes.
7. Pour the sauce over the lamb. Pipe or spoon the potatoes around the edge of the casserole dish and sprinkle the remaining cheese into the centre.
8. Return to the oven, uncovered, and cook for a further 20 minutes or until golden and bubbling. Garnish with a fresh rosemary sprig.

LAMB, LEEK & POTATO CASSEROLE S

Preparation time: 15 minutes
Cooking time: Low 8-10 hours
    High 4-5 hours

750 g/1½ lb potatoes, peeled
    and cut into 5 mm/¼ inch
    thick slices
2 medium leeks, thinly sliced
salt
freshly ground black pepper
½ teaspoon dried rosemary
2 tablespoons oil
8 large best end of neck lamb
    chops
300 ml/½ pint hot beef stock

1. Put the potatoes in a layer over the bottom of the stoneware pot. Add the leeks and sprinkle with a little salt and pepper and the rosemary.
2. Heat the oil in a frying pan. Add the chops and brown on both sides. Transfer the chops to the stoneware pot, arranging them so that the vegetables are completely covered. Add a little more salt and pepper and pour in the stock.
3. Cover and cook on Low for 8-10 hours or High for 4-5 hours.
4. Taste and adjust the seasoning before serving.

Top left: Lamb casserole
Top right: Scotch broth
Bottom left: Lamb, leek and potato casserole
Bottom right: Tomato lamb with cheese scalloped potatoes

SCOTCH BROTH

Preparation time: 20 minutes, plus soaking time
Cooking time: 2½ hours

1 kg/2 lb neck of lamb, sawn into pieces
1.5 litres/2½ pints light stock
salt
freshly ground black pepper
2 sticks celery, sliced
1 onion, peeled and sliced
1 small turnip, peeled and diced
1 carrot, scraped and sliced
2 leeks, white part only, sliced
1 bouquet garni
225 g/8 oz pearl barley, washed
50 g/2 oz dried butter beans, soaked in water overnight and drained
50 g/2 oz dried marrowfat peas, soaked in water overnight and drained
chopped fresh parsley, to garnish

Make sure that the lamb is sawn into pieces rather than chopped, which splinters the bones.

1. Put the lamb into a deep flameproof casserole, pour over the stock and season to taste with salt and pepper.
2. Bring slowly to the boil, skimming off the scum, then cover and simmer very gently for 1½ hours.
3. Lift out the lamb, remove the bones, dice the meat and return it to the pot with the remaining ingredients.
4. Cover and continue cooking for 1 hour or until the beans and peas are tender. Discard the bouquet garni. Adjust the seasoning.
5. Serve in deep soup plates, sprinkled generously with chopped parsley.

TOMATO LAMB WITH CHEESE SCALLOPED POTATOES P

Preparation time: 20 minutes
Cooking time: H pressure 15 minutes

2 tablespoons cooking oil
4 carrots, peeled and sliced
100 g/4 oz mushrooms, sliced
1 garlic clove, peeled and crushed
8 large best end lamb chops
1 × 400 g/14 oz can tomatoes
4 tablespoons water
1 bouquet garni
salt
freshly ground black pepper
750 g/1½ lb potatoes, peeled and thinly sliced
4 tablespoons single cream
little grated nutmeg
75 g/3 oz Cheddar cheese, grated
chopped fresh parsley, to garnish

1. Heat the oil in the open cooker. Add the carrots, mushrooms and garlic and fry until the carrots are beginning to colour. Lift out, draining well.
2. Add the chops to the cooker and brown on both sides. Return the fried vegetables to the cooker with the tomatoes and their juice, the water, bouquet garni and salt and pepper to taste.
3. Close the cooker, bring to H pressure and cook for 10 minutes. Reduce the pressure quickly.
4. Put the prepared potatoes in a separator with a little salt. Place on top of the chops.
5. Close the cooker again, bring to H pressure and cook for 5 minutes. Reduce the pressure quickly.
6. Lift out the potatoes and transfer half to a flameproof dish. Add half the cream, a little nutmeg and half the cheese. Cover with the remaining potatoes, a little more nutmeg and the remaining cheese. Brown the top under a hot grill.
7. Discard the bouquet garni from the lamb mixture and taste and adjust the seasoning. Transfer to a warmed serving dish. Sprinkle with a little parsley, and serve with the scalloped potatoes.

PORK & BROWN RICE PILAU

P

Preparation time: 12 minutes
Cooking time: H pressure 15 minutes

1 tablespoon vegetable oil
1 medium onion,
    peeled and chopped
1 garlic clove,
    peeled and crushed
1 green pepper,
    cored, seeded and chopped
100 g/4 oz mushrooms,
    quartered
275 g/10 oz brown rice
450 g/1 lb boned pork shoulder,
    cut into 2.5 cm/1 inch cubes
750 ml/1¼ pints chicken stock
2 tablespoons soy sauce
½ teaspoon dried thyme
salt
freshly ground black pepper

1. Heat the oil in the open cooker. Add the onion and garlic and fry until the onion is transparent. Stir in three-quarters of the green pepper and all of the mushrooms. Fry gently for 1 minute.
2. Add the rice and fry, stirring well, until all the oil is absorbed. Stir in the remaining ingredients, with salt and pepper to taste.
3. Close the cooker, bring to H pressure and cook for 15 minutes. Reduce the pressure quickly.
4. Remove the cover and stir the pilau thoroughly. If there is still some liquid, return the open cooker to a gentle heat and cook for a few minutes, stirring if necessary. Taste and adjust the seasoning.
5. Serve garnished with the reserved green pepper, very finely chopped.

PORK & BEAN HOTPOT

*Preparation time: 15 minutes, plus
soaking time*
Cooking time: H pressure 15 minutes

75 g/3 oz dried haricot beans
2 tablespoons oil
1 large onion, peeled and sliced
2 large carrots,
  scraped and sliced
450 g/1 lb boned pork shoulder,
  trimmed of excess fat and cut
  into 2.5 cm/1 inch cubes
2 tablespoons tomato purée
1 teaspoon dried mixed herbs
450 ml/¾ pint beef stock
salt
freshly ground black pepper

1. Put the haricot beans in a bowl, cover with boiling water and leave to soak for 1 hour. Drain the beans.
2. Heat the oil in the open cooker. Add the onion and carrots and fry until lightly browned. Lift out, draining well.
3. Add the pork to the cooker and brown on all sides. Remove the cooker from the heat and pour off any excess fat.
4. Return the vegetables to the cooker with the tomato purée, herbs, stock and salt and pepper to taste. Add the drained beans and stir well.
5. Close the cooker, bring to H pressure and cook for 15 minutes. Reduce the pressure slowly.
6. Taste and adjust the seasoning before serving.

PORK CASSEROLE WITH SAGE DUMPLINGS S

Preparation time: 15 minutes
Cooking time: Low 7-9 hours
  High 3½-4 hours

2 tablespoons oil
1 large onion, peeled and sliced
1 medium parsnip, peeled and
  cut into 1 cm/½ inch cubes
100 g/4 oz unsmoked bacon
  rashers, rind removed,
  chopped
750 g/1½ lb boned pork shoulder,
  trimmed of excess fat and cut
  into 2.5 cm/1 inch cubes
100 g/4 oz frozen or canned and
  drained sweetcorn kernels
450 ml/¾ pint chicken stock
salt
freshly ground black pepper
DUMPLINGS:
150 g/6 oz self-raising flour,
  sifted
75 g/3 oz shredded suet
½ teaspoon dried sage
salt
freshly ground black pepper
about 150 ml/¼ pint water

1. Heat the oil in a frying pan. Add the onion and parsnip and fry until they are lightly browned. Transfer to the stoneware pot.
2. Add the bacon and pork to the frying pan and brown evenly. Transfer to the stoneware pot and stir in the sweetcorn, stock and salt and pepper to taste.
3. Cover and cook on Low for 7-9 hours or High for 3½-4 hours.
4. To make the dumplings, mix together the flour, suet, sage and salt and pepper to taste. Add sufficient water to make a smooth dough that leaves the sides of the bowl clean.
5. Turn the dough out on to a floured surface. Divide into six pieces and form into balls.
6. If using the Low setting, turn to High 1 hour before the cooking time is completed.
7. At least 30 minutes before serving, drop the dumplings into the hot liquid. Cover again and continue cooking on High.

Below left: Pork and brown rice pilau
Below right: Pork and bean hotpot
Bottom: Pork casserole with sage dumplings

BRUNSWICK STEW

Preparation time: 30 minutes, plus soaking time
Cooking time: 2 hours
Oven: 160°C, 325°F, Gas Mark 3

3-4 tablespoons oil
100 g/4 oz streaky bacon, in the piece, rind removed, cubed
1 onion, peeled and chopped
50 g/2 oz plain flour
salt
freshly ground black pepper
1 rabbit, jointed
450 ml/¾ pint chicken stock
225 g/8 oz dried butter beans, soaked in water overnight and drained
1 tablespoon tomato purée
1 teaspoon finely chopped fresh savory, or ½ teaspoon dried savory

TOPPING:
75 g/3 oz butter
2 garlic cloves, peeled and crushed
4 thick slices French bread
1 tablespoon French mustard

chopped fresh parsley, to garnish

1. Heat the oil in a frying pan, add the bacon and cook over brisk heat for a few minutes. Transfer to a casserole.
2. Stir the onion into the oil and cook gently until softened. Add to the bacon.
3. Mix the flour with salt and pepper and use it to coat the rabbit joints. Add to the frying pan and brown lightly on all sides.
4. Transfer to the casserole. Stir any remaining seasoned flour into the fat in the frying pan and cook for 2 minutes.
5. Gradually stir in the stock and bring to the boil.
6. Add the beans, tomato purée and savory, and season to taste with salt and pepper. Pour into the casserole, cover and cook in a preheated oven for 2 hours or until the rabbit and beans are tender.
7. Fifteen minutes before the casserole is cooked, prepare the topping.
8. Melt the butter in a clean frying pan, add the garlic and bread and fry until the slices are golden on each side. Spread with the mustard.
9. Adjust the casserole seasoning, then arrange the mustard bread on top and sprinkle with parsley.

Right: Brunswick stew
Far right: Devilled veal

DEVILLED VEAL

Preparation time: 25 minutes
Cooking time: 1½ hours
Oven: 180°C, 350°F, Gas Mark 4

50 g/2 oz butter
750 g/1½ lb stewing veal, cubed
2 leeks, white part only, sliced
25 g/1 oz plain flour
350 ml/12 fl oz stock
225 g/8 oz parsnips, peeled and cubed
225 g/8 oz carrots, scraped and sliced
2 tablespoons tomato ketchup
2 teaspoons made mustard
2 teaspoons Worcestershire sauce
salt
freshly ground black pepper
225 g/8 oz tomatoes, skinned and sliced
4 streaky bacon rashers, rind removed, halved

TO GARNISH:
fried sliced mushrooms
chopped fresh parsley

1. Melt the butter in a flameproof casserole, add the veal and brown on all sides.
2. Stir in the leeks and cook gently for 5 minutes.
3. Mix in the flour and cook for 2 minutes. Stir in the stock and bring slowly to the boil.
4. Add the parsnips, carrots, tomato ketchup, mustard and Worcestershire sauce. Season to taste with salt and pepper.
5. Cover and transfer to a preheated oven. Cook for 1 hour.
6. Stir in the tomatoes. Roll up the bacon rashers and place on top of the casserole.
7. Return to the oven, uncovered, and continue cooking for 30 minutes or until the bacon rolls are crisp on top. Garnish with mushrooms and parsley.

Right: Puchero

PUCHERO

Preparation time: 1 hour 40 minutes, plus soaking time
Cooking time: 1¾ hours

100 g/4 oz dried chick peas, soaked in water overnight
225 g/8 oz chuck steak, cubed
4 chicken portions
225 g/8 oz boned lamb shoulder, cubed
piece of marrow bone
1 onion, peeled and chopped
1 garlic clove, peeled and crushed
2 carrots, scraped and sliced
beef stock
225 g/8 oz sweetcorn
1 small cabbage, quartered and cored
450 g/1 lb sweet potatoes, peeled and cubed
1 teaspoon chilli powder, or more, to taste
salt
freshly ground black pepper
25 g/1 oz butter
2 bananas, peeled and cut into thick, slanting slices
1 avocado, peeled, stoned and cut into thick slices
fresh coriander leaves, to garnish

In this recipe ordinary potatoes may be used in place of sweet potatoes. As chilli powder is very hot it should be used cautiously.

1. Drain the chick peas, put into a saucepan and cover with fresh cold water. Bring to the boil and simmer for 1 hour.
2. Drain again and put into a deep flameproof casserole with the steak, chicken, lamb, marrow bone, onion, garlic and carrots.
3. Just cover with beef stock and bring slowly to the boil. Cover and simmer very gently for 1 hour.
4. Add the sweetcorn, cabbage, sweet potatoes and chilli powder. Stir in a little more stock if necessary and season to taste with salt and pepper.
5. Re-cover and continue simmering for 45 minutes or until the meat and vegetables are tender.
6. Meanwhile, melt the butter in a large frying pan, add the banana and avocado slices and brown lightly. Transfer to a heated dish and keep hot.
7. Lift the chicken portions out of the casserole, remove the skin and bones and return the meat to the casserole.
8. Discard the marrow bone. Adjust the seasoning. Arrange the banana and avocado slices over the top and garnish with coriander.

SWEETBREADS WITH RICE

*Preparation time: 45 minutes, plus
   soaking time*
Cooking time: about 1 hour
Oven: 180°C, 350°F, Gas Mark 4

25 g/1 oz chicken fat or butter
450 g/1 lb sweetbreads
   (calf or lamb)
1 onion, peeled and finely
   chopped
100 g/4 oz Italian Piedmont rice
450 g/1 lb ripe tomatoes,
   skinned and sliced or,
   1 × 425 g/15 oz can peeled
   tomatoes, drained
150 ml/¼ pint dry white wine
300 ml/½ pint veal or chicken
   stock
1 bouquet garni
salt
freshly ground black pepper
2 tablespoons grated Parmesan
   cheese
4 streaky bacon rashers,
   rind removed
sprigs of watercress, to garnish

1. Soak the sweetbreads in cold water for several hours, changing the water as it becomes tinged with blood. Leave them until every trace of blood has disappeared, then place them in a pan.
2. Cover with cold water, bring to the boil and simmer for 3 minutes. Refresh under cold water and pat dry. Remove the fine skin and membranes. If using calves' sweetbreads, slice before using.
3. Melt the fat or butter in a frying pan, add the sweetbreads and brown lightly. Transfer to a casserole.
4. Add the onion to the pan and fry until softened.
5. Stir in the rice and cook for 5 minutes, then add the tomatoes, wine, stock and bouquet garni. Season to taste with salt and pepper.
6. Bring the mixture to the boil and pour it over the sweetbreads in the casserole.
7. Cover and cook in a preheated oven for 45 minutes or until the sweetbreads are tender.
8. Sprinkle the Parmesan cheese on both sides of the bacon rashers, pressing it on with a palette knife.
9. Discard the bouquet garni and adjust the seasoning, then arrange the rashers over the top of the sweetbreads.
10. Return to the oven, uncovered, and continue cooking for 15 minutes or until the topping is crisp and golden. Garnish with watercress.

BARBECUE CHICKEN WITH SAFFRON RICE   [P]

Preparation time: 10 minutes
Cooking time: H pressure 5 minutes

2 tablespoons oil
1 medium onion,
   peeled and chopped
4 chicken breasts, skinned
2 tablespoons tomato purée
3 tablespoons vinegar
3 tablespoons demerara sugar
2 teaspoons Worcestershire
   sauce
1 teaspoon dry mustard
300 ml/½ pint beef stock
salt
freshly ground black pepper
RICE:
225 g/8 oz long-grain rice
1 teaspoon salt
450 ml/¾ pint water
good pinch of powdered saffron
TO FINISH:
2 teaspoons cornflour
1 tablespoon cold water
chopped fresh parsley

1. Heat the oil in the open cooker. Add the onion and fry until lightly browned. Lift out, draining well.
2. Add the chicken breasts to the cooker and brown on all sides. Remove the cooker from the heat and drain off any excess oil.
3. Mix together the tomato purée, vinegar, sugar, Worcestershire sauce, mustard and stock. Pour over the chicken and return the onions to the cooker. Stir well.
4. Place the trivet over the chicken. Line the separator with foil, or use an ovenproof dish that will fit into the cooker. Put the rice, salt, water and saffron into the the separator or dish and place the container on top of the trivet.
5. Close the cooker, bring to H pressure and cook for 5 minutes. Reduce the pressure slowly.
6. Lift out the container. Tip the rice into a sieve and rinse with boiling water. Pile on to a large heated serving dish.
7. Lift out the chicken and arrange on the rice. Keep hot. Return the open cooker to the heat. Dissolve the cornflour in the cold water and add to the liquid in the cooker. Bring to the boil, stirring, and simmer until thickened. Taste and adjust the seasoning. Pour this sauce over the chicken and rice, then garnish with chopped parsley.

Above: Sweetbreads with rice

VEGETARIAN CASSEROLE

Preparation time: 45 minutes
Cooking time: 1½ hours
Oven: 160°C, 325°F, Gas Mark 3
*   220°C, 425°F, Gas Mark 7*

3 tablespoons olive or sunflower
    seed oil
1 onion, peeled and chopped
1 leek, sliced
2 carrots,
    lightly scraped and sliced
1 green pepper,
    cored, seeded and diced
1 red pepper,
    cored, seeded and diced
1 small celeriac, peeled and
    shredded
100 g/4 oz brown rice
450 ml/¾ pint vegetable stock
1 teaspoon yeast extract
    (optional)
salt
freshly ground black pepper
225 g/8 oz self-raising
    wholewheat flour
50 g/2 oz butter
50 g/2 oz Cheddar cheese,
    grated
25 g/1 oz walnuts, chopped
pinch of cayenne
1 egg, beaten
3-4 tablespoons milk,
    to mix and glaze
2 tablespoons toasted pumpkin
    seeds

1. Heat the oil in a flameproof casserole, add the onion and leek and cook for 5 minutes.
2. Stir in the carrots, peppers, celeriac and rice and cook for a further 5 minutes.
3. Add the stock and yeast extract, stir well and bring slowly to the boil. Season to taste with salt and pepper.
4. Cover the casserole and transfer to a preheated oven. Cook for 1¼ hours.
5. Meanwhile, prepare the topping. Put the flour into a bowl. Rub in the butter until the mixture resembles fine crumbs, then stir in the cheese and walnuts. Season with salt and cayenne pepper.
6. Add the egg and enough milk to mix to a fairly soft dough.

7. Pat out the dough on a floured board to about 2 cm/¾ inch thick and stamp out 5 cm/2 inch rounds. Brush the tops with milk.
8. Stir the pumpkin seeds into the casserole and adjust the seasoning.
9. Raise the oven temperature. Arrange the scones around the top of the casserole and return to the oven for a further 10-15 minutes, cooking or until well risen and golden brown.

Top: Vegetarian casserole
Bottom: Barbecue chicken
with saffron rice

PLAICE MORNAY PIE P

Preparation time: 20 minutes
Cooking time: H pressure 4 minutes

150 ml/¼ pint plus 3
   tablespoons milk
150 ml/¼ pint water
1 bay leaf
1 small onion,
   peeled and chopped
750 g/1½ lb potatoes, peeled
   and cut into small chunks
   (about 25 g/1 oz)
salt
8 small plaice fillets, skinned
freshly ground black pepper
25 g/1 oz margarine
good pinch of grated nutmeg
SAUCE:
25 g/1 oz margarine
25 g/1 oz plain flour
150 ml/¼ pint milk
75 g/3 oz Cheddar cheese,
   grated
salt
freshly ground black pepper

1. Put the 150 ml/¼ pint milk, the water, bay leaf and onion into the cooker. Add the trivet, rim side down. Pile the potatoes on the trivet and sprinkle with a little salt.
2. Put the fish fillets on a board, skinned side up, and season lightly with salt and pepper. Roll up from the tail end. Line the separator with a piece of greased foil. Put the fish rolls in the separator and place this on top of the potatoes.
3. Close the cooker, bring to H pressure and cook for 4 minutes. Reduce the pressure quickly.
4. Lift out the separator and transfer the fish rolls to a heated 900 ml/1½ pint pie dish. Keep hot.
5. Lift out the potatoes and place in a bowl. Add the margarine, remaining 3 tablespoons of milk and the nutmeg and mash until smooth. Keep hot.
6. Lift the trivet out of the cooker. Strain the liquid into a jug and reserve.
7. Return the rinsed cooker to the heat, and add the margarine. When melted, stir in the flour and cook for 1 minute. Remove the cooker from the heat and gradually stir in the reserved liquid and the additional milk. Return to the heat and bring to the boil, stirring. Add the cheese and season to taste with salt and pepper.
8. Pour the sauce over the fish, then carefully cover with the mashed potato. Decorate the top by marking with a fork or pipe on the potato.
9. Brown the potato under a hot grill and serve immediately.

COD & POTATO BAKE S

Preparation time: 15 minutes
Cooking time: Low 6-8 hours
     High 3-4 hours

50 g/2 oz butter or margarine
750 g/1½ lb potatoes,
   peeled and thinly sliced
1 medium onion,
   peeled and grated
1 medium green pepper,
   seeded and finely chopped
300 ml/½ pint hot chicken stock
½ teaspoon dried marjoram
500 g/1¼ lb cod fillets, skinned
   and cut into four portions
salt
freshly ground black pepper
50 g/2 oz Cheddar cheese,
   finely grated

1. Grease the stoneware pot with half the butter or margarine. Make a layer of potatoes over the bottom and scatter over the onion and pepper. Add the stock and marjoram.
2. Lay the pieces of fish on top and dot with the remaining butter or margarine. Season lightly with salt and pepper.
3. Cover and cook on Low for 6-8 hours or High for 3-4 hours.
4. One hour before serving, sprinkle the cheese over the fish.
5. If you have a removable stoneware pot, brown the cheese topping under a hot grill just before serving.

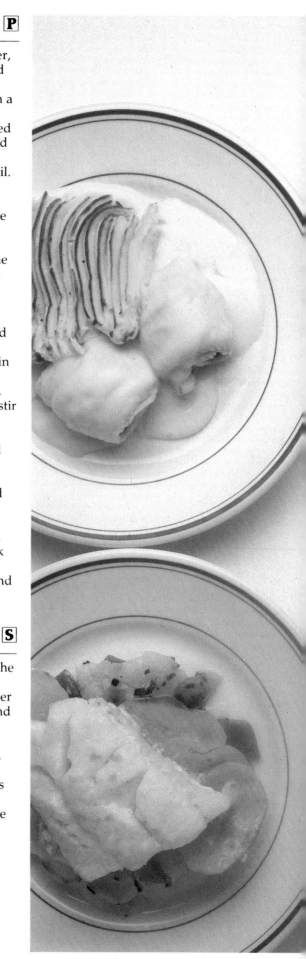

TUNA & CORN RISOTTO ⒮

Preparation time: 10 minutes
Cooking time: Low 3-4 hours
*   High 2-2½ hours*

1 garlic clove,
   peeled and crushed
1 medium onion,
   peeled and finely chopped
100 g/4 oz mushrooms,
   chopped
100 g/4 oz frozen or drained
   canned sweetcorn kernels
225 g/8 oz easy cook long-grain
   rice
½ teaspoon dried marjoram
900 ml/1½ pints hot chicken
   stock
salt
freshly ground black pepper
1 × 198 g/7 oz can tuna fish,
   drained and flaked into large
   pieces
1 tablespoon chopped fresh
   parsley

Only easy cook rice can be used for this recipe.

1. Put all the ingredients, except the parsley, into the stoneware pot. Stir well.
2. Cover and cook on Low for 3-4 hours or High for 2-2½ hours. Stir the mixture once during cooking to ensure that the liquid is absorbed evenly.
3. Before serving stir the chopped parsley into the risotto, and taste and adjust the seasoning.

FISH CASSEROLE

Preparation time: 35 minutes
Cooking time: 1¼ hours
Oven: 180°C, 350°F, Gas Mark 4

75 g/3 oz butter
2 leeks, white part only, sliced
750 g-1 kg/1½-2 lb mixed white
   fish fillets (cod, haddock,
   huss, whiting, coley or
   plaice), skinned and cut into 2
   inch pieces

PARSLEY SAUCE:
25 g/1 oz butter
25 g/1 oz plain flour
300 ml/½ pint milk, or
   chicken stock and milk
3 tablespoons chopped fresh
   parsley
2 teaspoons lemon juice
salt
freshly ground black pepper

2 hard-boiled eggs, chopped
½ teaspoon ground nutmeg
350 g/12 oz potatoes,
   peeled, cut into ¼ inch dice
   and blanched
2 tablespoons grated Parmesan
   cheese

1. Melt 50 g/2 oz of the butter in a frying pan, add the leeks and cook gently for 5 minutes.
2. Transfer the leeks to a lightly buttered casserole and cover with the fish.
3. To make the parsley sauce, melt the butter in a small saucepan. When foaming, stir in the flour and cook gently for 2 minutes. Gradually add the milk, stirring constantly, then bring to the boil and simmer for 10 minutes.
4. Stir in the parsley and lemon juice. Season to taste with salt and pepper.
5. Remove the pan from the heat, stir in the eggs and nutmeg, then adjust the seasoning.
6. Pour the sauce over the fish. Cover the casserole and cook in a preheated oven for 30 minutes.
7. Pat the potatoes dry with kitchen paper and place over the top of the fish. Season with salt and pepper.
8. Sprinkle with the Parmesan cheese and dot with the remaining butter. Return to the oven, uncovered, and cook for a further 30 minutes to brown the potatoes.

Top left: Plaice mornay pie
Top right: Tuna and corn risotto
Bottom left: Cod and potato bake
Bottom right: Fish casserole

AROUND THE WORLD

CHINESE LAMB

Preparation time: 40 minutes
Cooking time: 45 minutes
Oven: 180°C, 350°F, Gas Mark 4

8 lamb cutlets
50 g/2 oz seasoned flour
2 tablespoons oil
1 onion, peeled and chopped
450 ml/¾ pint stock
1 × 200 g/7 oz can bamboo
   shoots, drained and sliced
100 g/4 oz mushrooms, sliced
1 × 200 g/7 oz can water
   chestnuts, drained and sliced
2 sticks celery, sliced
2 tablespoons soy sauce
salt
freshly ground black pepper
spring onion brushes, to
   garnish
FRIED RICE:
2 spring onions, finely chopped
3 eggs, beaten
1 teaspoon salt
4 tablespoons oil
50 g/2 oz cooked ham, diced
100 g/4 oz peas, cooked
175 g/6 oz long-grain rice,
   cooked
1 tablespoon soy sauce

1. Coat the cutlets with the seasoned flour.
2. Heat the oil in a large frying pan, add the cutlets and brown well on each side. Transfer them to a casserole.
3. Add the onion to the frying pan and cook until golden. Stir in any remaining seasoned flour and cook for 2 minutes.
4. Stir in the stock and bring to the boil. Put the bamboo shoots, mushrooms, water chestnuts and celery into the casserole.
5. Add the soy sauce to the stock mixture, season to taste with salt and pepper and pour into the casserole.
6. Cover and cook in a preheated oven for 45 minutes or until the lamb is tender.
7. Meanwhile, make the fried rice. Mix half the spring onions with the eggs and a pinch of salt.
8. Heat a third of the oil in a frying pan, then add the eggs and stir until scrambled. Transfer to a warm plate and break up with a fork.
9. Heat the remaining oil in the pan. Add the remaining spring onions, the ham, peas, rice and soy sauce. Stir over the heat until hot.
10. Add the eggs, reduce the heat and cook for a further minute.
11. Garnish the lamb with spring onion brushes and serve with the fried rice, a small bowl of soy sauce and spring onions for dipping.

MALAYAN CHICKEN

*Preparation time: 1 hour, including
    side dishes*
Cooking time: 2½ hours

1 × 1½ kg/3½ lb boiling fowl,
    trussed
1 onion
chicken stock, to cover
salt
freshly ground black pepper
225 g/8 oz long-grain rice
40 g/1½ oz butter
2 teaspoons curry powder
40 g/1½ oz plain flour
150 ml/¼ pint milk
juice of ½ lemon
pinch of sugar
grated fresh coconut, to garnish

Traditionally, this dish is serve piled high with the accompaniments; however, it cools the chicken, which is not to English taste, so serve the accompaniments on separate dishes.

1. Place the chicken in a large flameproof casserole, add the unpeeled onion and enough stock to cover the bird. Season with a little salt and pepper.
2. Bring to the boil slowly, skimming off the scum, then cover and simmer for 1½ hours or until absolutely tender.
3. Lift the chicken on to a board.
4. Skim the fat from the stock and discard the onion, then bring it back to the boil.
5. Add the rice and cook until tender.
6. Meanwhile, remove the trussing string and skin from the chicken. Take the meat from the bones, cut into bite-size pieces and reserve.
7. Drain the rice, reserving the stock, and place the rice in a heated serving dish. Keep hot.
8. Melt the butter in a saucepan, add the curry powder and cook for 5 minutes.
9. Stir in the flour and cook for 2 minutes.
10. Gradually stir in the milk and 150 ml/¼ pint of the reserved stock. Bring to the boil. Season to taste with salt and pepper, and stir in the lemon juice and sugar.
11. Fold in the chicken meat and reheat carefully, then pour over the rice.
12. Garnish with fresh coconut, and serve with a good selection from the following: chopped pineapple (fresh or canned), thinly sliced celery, sliced hard-boiled egg, salted peanuts, sliced bananas, diced cucumber in unsweetened plain yogurt, finely chopped onion.

NASI GORENG

Preparation time: 40 minutes
Cooking time: 1¾ hours
Oven: 160℃, 325°F, Gas Mark 3

6 tablespoons oil
750 g/1½ lb boned pork shoulder,
   cubed
2 onions, peeled and chopped
2 garlic cloves,
   peeled and crushed
1 bay leaf
6 parsley stalks
350 ml/12 fl oz stock
salt
freshly ground black pepper
225 g/8 oz long-grain rice
100 g/4 oz peeled shrimps
1 teaspoon ground coriander
large pinch of cayenne
½ teaspoon ground cumin
½ teaspoon ground nutmeg
2 tablespoons peanut butter
TO GARNISH:
tomato wedges
salted peanuts
or cooked omelette strips

1. Heat 2 tablespoons of the oil in a flameproof casserole, add the pork and brown well.
2. Add the onions and cook gently until softened. Stir in the garlic, bay leaf, parsley stalks and stock. Season to taste with salt and pepper.
3. Bring to the boil, then cover and transfer to a preheated oven. Cook for 1¼-1½ hours or until the pork is tender.
4. Meanwhile, bring a large saucepan of water to the boil, salt lightly, add the rice and simmer for 15 minutes or until tender. Drain well.
5. Heat the remaining 4 tablespoons of oil in a large frying pan, add the rice and fry for 5 minutes, turning over well.
6. Stir in the shrimps and spices and heat through gently.
7. Stir the peanut butter into the casserole and adjust the seasoning. Discard the bay leaf. Pour into a heated deep serving dish.
8. Pile the fried rice over the top. Garnish with tomato wedges and peanuts or omelette strips.

Far left: Malayan chicken
Left: Nasi goreng

CHICKEN KORMA P

Preparation time: 10 minutes
Cooking time: H pressure 8 minutes

2 tablespoons cooking oil
1 large onion, peeled and sliced
1 garlic clove,
   peeled and crushed
4 chicken quarters, skinned
1 tablespoon mild curry powder
1 × 400 g/14 oz can tomatoes,
   chopped, with their juice
150 ml/¼ pint chicken stock
2 teaspoons lemon juice
1 bay leaf
salt
150 ml/¼ pint plain
   unsweetened yogurt

1. Heat the oil in the open cooker. Add the onion and garlic and fry until the onion is transparent. Lift out, draining well.
2. Add the chicken pieces to the cooker and brown on all sides. Lift out.
3. Add the curry powder to the remaining oil in the cooker and fry gently for 2 minutes. Remove the cooker from the heat and return the onion, garlic and chicken to the cooker with the tomatoes, stock, lemon juice, bay leaf and salt to taste. Stir well.
4. Close the cooker, bring to H pressure and cook for 8 minutes. Reduce the pressure quickly.
5. Remove the bay leaf. Stir in the yogurt, taste and adjust the seasoning. Serve with plain boiled rice and other curry accompaniments of your choice.

Left: Chicken korma

TURKISH PILAFF

Preparation time: 20 minutes
Cooking time: 1 hour 10 minutes
Oven: 160°C, 325°F, Gas Mark 3

100 g/4 oz butter
1 large onion,
    peeled and finely chopped
450 g/1 lb cooked lamb, cubed
225 g/8 oz long-grain rice
½ teaspoon saffron powder
600 ml/1 pint chicken stock
2 tablespoons chopped fresh
    parsley
1 teaspoon ground allspice
salt
freshly ground black pepper
50 g/2 oz blanched almonds,
    chopped and lightly toasted
TO GARNISH:
fried aubergine slices
chopped parsley

1. Melt 50 g/2 oz of the butter in a flameproof casserole, add the onion and cook gently until softened.
2. Stir in the lamb and rice and cook for 5 minutes, stirring well.
3. Dissolve the saffron in a little boiling water and stir into the stock. Add to the casserole with the parsley and allspice.
4. Mix well and season to taste with salt and pepper. Bring to the boil.
5. Tuck greased greaseproof paper over the rice mixture, then cover the casserole and cook in a preheated oven for about 1 hour or until the rice has absorbed the stock and is tender.
6. With a fork, gently turn over the rice to mix in the almonds and the remaining 50 g/ 2 oz butter. Adjust the seasonings. Garnish with aubergine slices and parsley.

HUNGARIAN CHICKEN

Preparation time: 30 minutes
Cooking time: 1½ hours

1 tablespoon oil
4 streaky bacon rashers,
    rind removed, quartered
1 large onion, peeled and sliced
1 tablespoon sweet Hungarian
    paprika
1 × 1½ kg/3½ lb roasting chicken,
    jointed
300 ml/½ pint chicken stock
salt
freshly ground black pepper
1 teaspoon chopped fresh basil
    or ½ teaspoon dried basil
225 g/8 oz smoked sausage,
    sliced
1 green pepper,
    cored, seeded, and sliced
225 g/8 oz green beans,
    cut into 2inch lengths
2 tablespoons tomato ketchup
TO GARNISH:
thin red pepper rings
chopped fresh parsley

1. Heat the oil in a flameproof casserole, add the bacon and onion and cook for 5 minutes. Stir in the paprika and cook for 2 minutes.
2. Put the chicken joints into the pot, turn them over to coat with the paprika and cook for 5 minutes. Pour in the chicken stock, season to taste with salt and pepper and add the basil.
3. Bring to the boil, then cover and simmer very gently for 1 hour, basting the chicken with the sauce from time to time.
4. Stir in the sausage, green pepper, beans and tomato ketchup. Adjust the seasoning.
5. Re-cover and continue simmering for 30 minutes
6. Turn into a heated serving dish and garnish with red pepper rings and parsley.

Top left: Turkish pilaff
Top right: Frikadeller
Bottom left: Hungarian chicken
Bottom right: Sauerkraut and pork goulash

FRIKADELLER

Preparation time: 45 minutes
Cooking time: 1 hour
Oven: 160°C, 325°F, Gas Mark 3

450 g/1 lb minced veal
50 g/2 oz pork fat, diced
2 anchovy fillets
1 onion, peeled and chopped
1 × 100 g/4 oz slice brown bread,
　crusts removed
2 tablespoons milk
4 tablespoons cold water
salt
freshly ground black pepper
50 g/2 oz seasoned flour
3 tablespoons oil
SAUCE:
25 g/1 oz butter
1 small onion,
　peeled and finely chopped
25 g/1 oz plain flour
250 ml/8 fl oz veal or chicken
　stock
2 garlic cloves,
　peeled and crushed
1 × 425 g/15 oz can tomatoes,
　chopped, with their juice
1 bouquet garni
150 ml/¼ pint plain
　unsweetened yogurt
TO GARNISH:
black olives
lemon twists
sprigs of parsley

1. Pass the veal, pork fat, anchovy fillets and onion through the fine blade of the mincer.
2. Soak the bread in the milk and squeeze dry. Work the bread into the meat mixture with a wet hand. Incorporate the water a little at a time, and season with salt and pepper.
3. Form the mixture into 8 small balls and coat with the seasoned flour.
4. Heat the oil in a large frying pan, add the veal balls and brown them on all sides. Transfer to a casserole.
5. To make the sauce, melt the butter in a saucepan, add the onion and cook until softened. Stir in the flour and cook for 2 minutes.
6. Gradually stir in the stock and bring to the boil, stirring. Add the garlic, tomatoes, and the bouquet garni. Season to taste with salt and pepper.
7. Pour the sauce over the veal balls, cover the casserole and cook in a preheated oven for 55 minutes.
8. Stir the yogurt very carefully into the sauce; do not break the veal balls. Adjust the seasoning.
9. Discard the bouquet garni. Garnish with olives, lemon twists and parsley sprigs.

SAUERKRAUT & PORK GOULASH

Preparation time: 20 minutes
Cooking time: about 2½ hours
Oven: 160°C, 325°F, Gas Mark 3
*　　150°C, 300°F, Gas Mark 2*

2 tablespoons oil
2 onions,
　peeled and finely chopped
1 tablespoon paprika
750 g/1½ lb boned pork shoulder,
　cubed
600 ml/1 pint chicken stock
salt
freshly ground black pepper
1 × 425 g/15 oz can sauerkraut,
　well rinsed under cold
　running water and drained
2 teaspoons caraway seeds
150 ml/¼ pint soured cream
sprigs of fresh sage, to garnish

1. Heat the oil in a flameproof casserole, add the onions and cook until golden brown. Stir in the paprika and cook for 2 minutes.
2. Add the pork, turn it over to coat with the paprika and pour in 300 ml/½ pint of the stock. Season to taste with salt and pepper.
3. Bring to the boil, then cover and transfer to a preheated oven. Cook for 1 hour.
4. Stir in the sauerkraut, caraway seeds and the remaining 300 ml/½ pint stock, and adjust the seasoning.
5. Re-cover, return to the oven, reducing the temperature and continue cooking for 1-1½ hours or until the pork is very tender and the stock has been absorbed.
6. Do not allow the goulash to dry out; add a little more stock if necessary.
7. Stir in the soured cream and adjust the seasoning. Turn into a heated serving dish, garnish with sage and accompany with Sausage Meat Balls (page 141).

PORK CHOPS ARDENNAISE S

Preparation time: 18 minutes, plus marinating time
Cooking time: Low 7-9 hours
High 3-4 hours

225 g/8 oz gammon rasher, rind removed, cut into thin strips
175 g/6 oz shallots, or small onions, peeled
300 ml/½ pint dry white wine
25 g/1 oz butter or margarine
4 pork loin chops
100 g/4 oz button mushrooms
salt
freshly ground black pepper
1 tablespoon cornflour
1 tablespoon French mustard
1½ tablespoons cold water
150 ml/¼ pint single cream
chopped fresh parsley, to garnish

1. Put the gammon, shallots and wine into a bowl and leave to marinate for at least 1 hour.
2. Melt the butter or margarine in a frying pan. Add the chops and brown on both sides. Transfer to the stoneware pot and add the mushrooms.
3. Drain off the wine from the shallots and gammon and pour into the stoneware pot.
4. Add the shallots and gammon to the frying pan and fry until both are beginning to brown. Transfer to the stoneware pot and add a little salt and pepper.
5. Cover and cook on Low for 7-9 hours or High for 3-4 hours.
6. Mix together the cornflour, mustard and cold water. Lift out two of the chops and stir the cornflour mixture into the liquid until thickened. Stir in the cream and taste and adjust the seasoning. Return the two chops and baste with the sauce.
7. Just before serving sprinkle with chopped parsley.

PAUPIETTES DE VEAU S

Preparation time: 15 minutes
Cooking time: Low 7-9 hours
High 3-4 hours

4 veal escalopes, about 100 g/4 oz each
4 unsmoked bacon rashers, rind removed, finely chopped
1 tablespoon chopped fresh parsley
1 garlic clove, peeled and crushed
50 g/2 oz fresh white breadcrumbs
1 egg, beaten
salt
freshly ground black pepper
2 tablespoons cooking oil
100 g/4 oz mushrooms, sliced
1 × 225 g/8 oz can tomatoes, chopped, with their juice
150 ml/¼ pint hot chicken stock
8 stuffed green olives, sliced
1 tablespoon cornflour
1½ tablespoons cold water

1. Beat the escalopes with a rolling pin or meat mallet until they are thin.
2. Mix together the bacon, parsley, garlic, breadcrumbs and beaten egg. Season with salt and pepper.
3. Divide the stuffing between the escalopes and spread almost to the edges. Roll up tightly and secure with string or cotton thread.
4. Heat the oil in a frying pan. Add the veal rolls and fry until browned on all sides. Transfer to the stoneware pot.
5. Add the mushrooms, tomatoes, stock, olives and a little salt and pepper to the frying pan. Bring to the boil, stirring, and pour over the veal.
6. Cover and cook on Low for 7-9 hours or High for 3-4 hours.
7. Lift out the veal rolls and remove the strings. Dissolve the cornflour in the cold water and stir into the sauce until thickened. Return the veal rolls to the pot, baste well with the sauce and reheat for a few minutes. Taste and adjust the seasoning before serving. The bacon may have tinged the veal pink, but this does not mean it isn't cooked.

Above left: Pork chops ardennaise
Above right: Normandy apple pudding
Above centre: Paupiettes de veau

NORMANDY APPLE PUDDING   P

Preparation time: 20 minutes, plus chilling time
Cooking time: H pressure 6 minutes

50 g/2 oz butter or margarine
50 g/2 oz caster sugar
1 egg, beaten
225 g/8 oz plain sponge cake
    crumbs
450 g/1 lb cooking apples,
    peeled, cored and sliced
3 tablespoons brandy
3 tablespoons granulated sugar
600 ml/1 pint hot water
whipped cream, to serve

1. Cream together the butter or margarine and caster sugar until light and fluffy. Add the egg a little at a time. Stir in the cake crumbs.
2. Lightly grease a 1.2 litre/2 pint soufflé dish. Make a layer of about half of the apples over the bottom of the dish and sprinkle with half the brandy and 1 tablespoon of the granulated sugar.
3. Cover with half the creamed mixture, then repeat these two layers again.
4. Cover the dish with a piece of greased foil or double thickness of greased greaseproof paper. Tie on securely.

5. Put the trivet into the cooker, rim side down, and pour in the hot water. Stand the covered dish on the trivet.
6. Close the cooker, bring to H pressure and cook for 6 minutes. Reduce the pressure quickly.
7. Lift out the pudding and remove the covering. Sprinkle with the remaining tablespoon of granulated sugar.
8. Place under a hot grill and cook until the sugar begins to caramelize. Chill well before serving, with whipped cream.

PORTUGUESE CABBAGE & POTATO SOUP   P

Serves 4-6
Preparation time: 10 minutes
Cooking time: H pressure 5 minutes

2 tablespoons olive oil
3 medium potatoes,
   peeled and sliced
1 medium onion,
   peeled and chopped
1 small green cabage,
   cored and finely shredded
900 ml/1½ pints chicken stock
salt
freshly ground black pepper

1. Heat the oil in the open cooker. Add the potatoes and onion and fry until the onion is transparent.
2. Add the cabbage, reserving 2 tablespoons for the garnish. Cook until the cabbage is beginning to soften.
3. Stir in the stock and salt and pepper to taste.
4. Close the cooker, bring to H pressure and cook for 5 minutes. Reduce the pressure quickly.
5. Purée the soup in a blender or press through a sieve.
6. Return the soup to the open cooker and add the reserved shredded raw cabbage. Bring to the boil and simmer, stirring occasionally, for 3 minutes. Taste and adjust the seasoning before serving.

CATAPLANA

Preparation time: 10 minutes
Cooking time: H pressure 15 minutes

1 tablespoon olive oil
1 large onion,
    peeled and chopped
2 garlic cloves,
    peeled and crushed
750 g/1½ lb lean boned pork,
    cut into 2.5 cm/1 inch cubes
450 ml/¾ pint white wine
½ teaspoon dried thyme
salt
freshly ground black pepper
TO FINISH:
1 × 225 g/8 oz can mussels,
    drained
2 teaspoons cornflour
1 tablespoon cold water
chopped fresh parsley

Cataplana is one of the best known regional dishes of the Algarve in Portugal. Traditionally it is cooked in a very primitive type of pressure cooker which looks like two dustbin lids locked together.

1. Heat the oil in the open cooker. Add the onion and garlic and fry until the onion is lightly browned. Lift out, draining well.
2. Add the pork to the cooker and brown on all sides. Return the onion and garlic to the cooker with the wine, thyme and salt and pepper to taste. Stir well.
3. Close the cooker, bring to H pressure and cook for 15 minutes. Reduce the pressure quickly.
4. Return the open cooker to the heat. Stir in the mussels and simmer gently for 5 minutes. Dissolve the cornflour in the cold water and stir into the Cataplana until thickened. Taste and adjust the seasoning.
5. Sprinkle with parsley and serve with plain boiled rice.

FABADA

Preparation time: 2½ hours,
    plus soaking time
Cooking time: 2 hours
Oven: 160°C, 325°F, Gas Mark 3

350 g/12 oz dried haricot beans,
    soaked in water overnight
2 tablespoons oil
1 × 450 g/1 lb bacon joint,
    cubed
450 g/1 lb boned leg of lamb,
    cubed
2 onions, peeled and chopped
900 ml/1½ pints stock
1 bouquet garni
2 garlic cloves,
    peeled and crushed
2 tablespoons tomato purée
salt
freshly ground black pepper
225 g/8 oz black pudding,
    skinned and sliced (optional)
sprigs of fresh thyme, to garnish

This is a peasant dish from northern Spain.

1. Drain the beans, put them into a saucepan and cover with fresh cold water. Bring to the boil and simmer for about 2 hours.
2. Meanwhile, heat the oil in a flameproof casserole, add the bacon and lamb cubes and brown on all sides. Add the onions and cook gently until softened.
3. Add the stock, bouquet garni, garlic and tomato purée. Season to taste with salt and pepper, and bring slowly to the boil.
4. Cover and transfer to a preheated oven. Cook for 1 hour.
Drain the beans, add to the casserole and stir well. Re-cover and cook for a further 1 hour or until the meat and beans are tender and the dish is 'creamy'.
6. Stir in the black pudding and heat through gently.
7. Discard the bouquet garni, taste and adjust the seasoning then garnish with fresh thyme.

Below left: Portuguese cabbage and potato soup
Below right: Cataplana
Bottom: Fabada

BEAN & TUNA ANTIPASTO P

Preparation time: 10 minutes, plus
soaking time
Cooking time: H pressure 15 minutes

225 g/8 oz dried haricot beans
900 ml/1½ pints cold water
1 large onion,
   peeled and chopped
¼ teaspoon dried mixed herbs
3 tablespoons olive oil
1 tablespoon wine vinegar
salt
freshly ground black pepper
2 × 198 g/7 oz cans tuna fish,
   drained and flaked into large
   pieces
1 tablespoon chopped fresh
   parsley
12 black olives, stoned

1. Place the beans in a large bowl and cover with boiling water. Soak for 1 hour, then drain.
2. Put the beans into the cooker with the cold water, onion and herbs.
3. Close the cooker, bring to H pressure and cook for 15 minutes. Reduce the pressure slowly.
4. Drain the beans and chill thoroughly.
5. Mix together the oil, vinegar and salt and pepper to taste. Toss the beans in the dressing, then carefully fold in the tuna fish, parsley and olives.

COD ALLA ROMANA S

Preparation time: 15 minutes
Cooking time: Low 4-6 hours
   High 2-3 hours

1 tablespoon cooking oil
1 small onion,
   peeled and thinly sliced
1 garlic clove, crushed

1 green pepper, cored, seeded
   and thinly sliced
750 g/1½ lb cod fillet, skinned
   and cut into 2.5 cm/1 inch wide
   strips
1 × 400 g/14 oz can tomatoes,
   chopped, with their juice
½ teaspoon dried basil
12 black olives, stoned
salt
freshly ground black pepper

1. Heat the oil in a frying pan. Add the onion, garlic and green peppers and fry until lightly browned. Transfer to the stoneware pot, draining well.
2. Add the fish to the frying pan and brown very lightly. Lay the fish on top of the vegetables in the stoneware pot.
3. Add the tomatoes, basil, olives and salt and pepper to taste to the pot.
4. Cover and cook on Low for 4-6 hours or High for 2-3 hours.
5. Taste and adjust the seasoning, then serve with thickly sliced French bread or boiled potatoes.

Right: Bean and tuna antipasto
Far right: Cod alla romana

Below: Sicilian peaches

SICILIAN PEACHES S

Serves 6
Preparation time: 20 minutes,
* plus soaking time*
Cooking time: Low 4-6 hours
* High 2-3 hours*

25 g/1 oz butter
50 g/2 oz caster sugar
1 egg, beaten
100 g/4 oz macaroons, crushed
few drops of almond essence
6 large peaches,
  skinned, halved and stoned
150 ml/¼ pint water
50 g/2 oz granulated sugar
whipped cream, to serve

1. Cream together the butter and caster sugar. Mix in the egg, macaroons and almond essence.
2. Fill the peach halves with the macaroon mixture.
3. Put the water and granulated sugar in the stoneware pot and stir to dissolve the sugar. Place the peaches carefully in the syrup.
4. Cover and cook on Low for 4-6 hours or High for 2-3 hours.
5. Chill well before serving, with whipped cream.

BAMIA & LAMB CASSEROLE

Preparation time: 30 minutes
Cooking time: 1½ hours
Oven: 160°C, 325°F, Gas Mark 3

50 g/2 oz butter
2 onions, peeled and chopped
2 garlic cloves,
    peeled and crushed
750 g/1½ lb boned lamb
    shoulder, cubed
450 g/1 lb okra (ladies' fingers),
    stems removed
450 g/1 lb ripe tomatoes,
    skinned, seeded and diced or
    1 × 425 g/15 oz can tomatoes,
    drained
1 teaspoon ground coriander
300 ml/½ pint stock
salt
freshly ground black pepper
juice of 1 lime or lemon
150 ml/¼ pint plain
    unsweetened yogurt
blanched shreds of lime or
    lemon rind, to garnish

Bamia is the Creole word for okra.

1. Melt the butter in a flameproof casserole, add the onions and cook gently until softened.
2. Stir in the garlic and lamb and continue cooking until the lamb is lightly browned.
3. Add the okra and turn it over in the butter. Stir in the tomatoes, coriander and stock. Season to taste with salt and pepper.
4. Bring to the boil, then cover and transfer to a preheated oven. Cook for 1 hour.
5. Stir in the lime or lemon juice. Cook for a further 30 minutes or until the lamb is very tender.
6. Gently stir in the yogurt. Adjust the seasoning. Turn into a heated serving dish and sprinkle with shreds of lime or lemon rind. Serve with new potatoes.

JAMBALAYA [S]

Preparation time: 15 minutes
Cooking time: Low 4-5 hours
*   High 2-2½ hours*

2 tablespoons vegetable oil
1 large onion,
    peeled and chopped
1 garlic clove,
    peeled and crushed
1 green pepper,
    cored, seeded and chopped
225 g/8 oz easy cook long-grain
    rice
100 g/4 oz salami,
    cut into small cubes
100 g/4 oz shelled cooked
    prawns
100 g/4 oz cooked chicken meat,
    diced
1 bay leaf
1 teaspoon dried thyme
salt
freshly ground black pepper
450 ml/¾ pint hot chicken stock
300 ml/½ pint dry white wine

Only easy cook rice may be used for this recipe. For best results do not exceed the maximum cooking time given.

1. Heat the oil in a frying pan. Add the onion, garlic and green pepper and fry until softened. Transfer to the stoneware pot and add the remaining ingredients. Stir well.
2. Cover and cook on Low for 4-5 hours or High for 2-2½ hours. Stir once during cooking to ensure even absorption of the liquid.
3. Discard the bay leaf, and taste and adjust the seasoning before serving.

Top left: Bamia and lamb casserole
Top right: Mexican chick pea casserole
Centre: Jambalaya
Bottom: New England chowder

MEXICAN CHICK PEA CASSEROLE S

Preparation time: 20 minutes,
  plus soaking time
Cooking time: Low 8-10 hours
  High 4-5 hours

100 g/4 oz dried chick peas
2 tablespoons cooking oil
2 medium onions,
  peeled and sliced
1 garlic clove,
  peeled and crushed
2 unsmoked bacon rashers,
  rind removed, chopped
750 g/1½ lb boned pork shoulder,
  trimmed of excess fat and
  cubed
1 × 225 g/8 oz can red
  pimento, drained and sliced
1 tablespoon tomato purée
1 teaspoon mild chilli powder
300 ml/½ pint hot beef stock
salt
2 teaspoons cornflour
1 tablespoon cold water
chopped fresh parsley, to
  garnish

1. Put the chick peas in a saucepan, cover with cold water and bring to the boil. Simmer for 10 minutes, then remove from the heat and leave to soak for at least 1 hour. Drain. (This step can be completed the night before.)
2. Heat the oil in a frying pan. Add the onions and garlic and fry until light golden brown. Transfer to the stoneware pot.
3. Fry the bacon and pork in the same pan until lightly browned. Transfer to the stoneware pot and add the pimento and chick peas.
4. Mix together the tomato purée, chilli powder and hot stock. Stir into the other ingredients in the pot and season to taste with salt.
5. Cover and cook on Low for 8-10 hours or High for 4-5 hours.
6. Dissolve the cornflour in the cold water and stir into the mixture in the pot until thickened. Taste and adjust the seasoning.
7. Garnish with a little chopped parsley before serving.

NEW ENGLAND CHOWDER P

Preparation time: 10 minutes
Cooking time: H pressure 3 minutes

1 tablespoon cooking oil
2 unsmoked bacon rashers,
  rind removed, chopped
1 medium onion,
  peeled and chopped
2 celery sticks, finely chopped
350 g/12 oz potatoes, peeled
  and cut into 1 cm/½ inch dice
350 g/12 oz cod fillets, skinned
  and cut into 2.5 cm/1 inch
  pieces
600 ml/1 pint chicken stock or
  water
¼ teaspoon ground turmeric
¼ teaspoon dried thyme
1 bay leaf
freshly ground black pepper
TO FINISH:
1 × 290 g/10 oz can baby clams
  or mussels, drained
150 ml/¼ pint single cream
1 tablespoon chopped fresh
  parsley

1. Heat the oil in the open cooker. Add the bacon and fry gently for 1 minute. Add the onion, celery and potato and fry until the onion is transparent. Lift out, draining well.
2. Add the cod to the cooker and fry until lightly browned. Lift out and drain off any excess oil
3. Return the vegetables, bacon and fish to the cooker with the stock or water, turmeric, thyme, bay leaf and pepper to taste. Stir well.
4. Close the cooker, bring to H pressure and cook for 3 minutes. Reduce the pressure quickly.
5. Return the open cooker to the heat. Add the drained clams or mussels and simmer for 3-4 minutes. Discard the bay leaf.
6. Just before serving stir in the cream and parsley, and taste and adjust the seasoning.

VEGETABLES

BRAISED LETTUCE

Preparation time: 10 minutes
Cooking time: 1 hour
Oven: 150°C, 300°F, Gas Mark 2

4 large lettuces, trimmed
salt
freshly ground black pepper
50 g/2 oz butter
1 onion, peeled and sliced
1 carrot, scraped and sliced
2 bacon rashers, rind removed,
    blanched and halved
300 ml/½ pint chicken stock
bouquet garni
chopped fresh parsley,
    to garnish

This recipe is particularly useful at the end of the summer when the garden lettuces are past their prime.

1. Blanch the whole lettuces in boiling, lightly salted water for 3 minutes. Plunge them into cold water. Drain.
2. Press out as much water as possible, cut the lettuces in half lengthways and fold in half.
3. Melt 25 g/1 oz of the butter in a frying pan, and cook the onion and carrot gently for 5 minutes. Place on the bottom of a flameproof casserole, arrange the folded lettuce on top and cover with the bacon.
4. Add the stock to the pan, bring to the boil, season with salt and pepper, then pour over the casserole and tuck the bouquet garni down the side.
5. Cover closely with the buttered paper and lid, and cook in a preheated oven for 1 hour.
6. Lift the lettuce on to a heated serving dish and cover with bacon.
7. Strain the sauce into a small pan, bring to the boil, reduce a little, remove and flake in the remaining butter. Shake the pan to blend well then pour over the lettuce.
8. Sprinkle with chopped parsley and serve with braised meats or fish.

STUFFED SPANISH ONIONS

S

Preparation time: 20 minutes
Cooking time: Low 8-10 hours
  High 4-5 hours

4 medium Spanish onions,
  peeled
25 g/1 oz butter or margarine
3 smoked bacon rashers,
  rind removed, finely chopped
50 g/2 oz mushrooms,
  finely chopped
25 g/2 oz fresh breadcrumbs
salt
freshly ground black pepper
300 ml/½ pint hot beef stock

1. Put the onions in a saucepan, cover with water and bring to the boil. Simmer for 5 minutes, then drain well.
2. Melt the butter or margarine in a frying pan. Add the bacon and mushrooms and fry gently for 2 minutes. Stir in the breadcrumbs and continue frying until the breadcrumbs are pale golden brown. Season well with salt and pepper. Remove from the heat.
3. Using an apple corer or sharp knife, remove the centre from each onion, making a hole about 2.5 cm/1 inch in diameter.

4. Fill the centre of each onion with the bacon mixture, pressing it down well.
5. Stand the stuffed onions in the stoneware pot and pour the hot stock around them.
6. Cover and cook on Low for 8-10 hours or High for 4-5 hours. Serve as a supper dish.

Right: Stuffed Spanish onions
Below left: Meat dolmas
Below right: Braised celery

BRAISED CELERY

Preparation time: 15 minutes
Cooking time: about 1½ hours
Oven: 160°C, 325°F, Gas Mark 3

2 large heads of celery, trimmed
    to 20 cm/8 inch lengths, and
    halved lengthwise.
100 g/4 oz bacon trimmings and
    rinds
1 onion, peeled and sliced
1 carrot, scraped and sliced
bouquet garni
300 ml/½ pint hot vegetable
    stock
squeeze of lemon juice
salt
freshly ground black pepper
celery leaves, to garnish

1. Put the celery into a pan of cold water and bring to the boil. Boil for 5 minutes, strain and refresh under cold water. Drain well.
2. Place the bacon on the bottom of a casserole and cover with the slices of onion and carrot. Lay the celery on top with a bouquet garni, pour over the stock and lemon juice, and season with salt and pepper.
3. Cover closely with greased paper and a lid and cook in a preheated oven for 1½ hours, or until the celery is tender. Arrange in a heated serving dish.
4. Strain the sauce into a small pan, bring to the boil and pour over the celery.
5. Garnish with the celery leaves and serve with roast beef or pork.

MOCK DOLMAS   [S]

Preparation time: 20 minutes
Cooking time: Low 6-8 hours
   High 3-4 hours

75 g/3 oz long-grain rice
12 large cabbage leaves
100 g/4 oz cooked shoulder
    ham, chopped
1 hard-boiled egg, chopped
¼ teaspoon grated nutmeg
salt
freshly ground black pepper
1 × 400 g/14 oz can tomatoes,
    chopped, with their juice

1. Cook the rice in boiling salted water in a saucepan for about 10 minutes or until tender. Drain in a sieve, if necessary, and rinse with boiling water.
2. Blanch the cabbage leaves in boiling water for 1 minute. Drain and pat dry with paper towels.
3. Mix together the cooked rice, ham, egg, nutmeg and salt and pepper to taste. Divide equally between the cabbage leaves, placing the filling in the centre. Fold over the edges of the leaves and the stalk end, then roll up to form parcels, enclosing the filling.
4. Place the rolls in the stoneware pot. Pour over the tomatoes.
5. Cover and cook on Low for 6-8 hours of High for 3-4 hours. Serve as a supper dish.

CURRIED FRUIT CASSEROLE

Preparation time: 30 minutes
Cooking time: 45 minutes
Oven: 160°C, 325°F, Gas Mark 3

2 tablespoons grated fresh or
    desiccated coconut
4 tablespoons boiling water
50 g/2 oz butter
2 onions, peeled and sliced
1 tablespoon curry paste
25 g/1 oz plain flour
300 ml/½ pint vegetable stock
2 teaspoons apricot jam
1 teaspoon lemon juice
salt
freshly ground black pepper
2 large bananas,
    peeled and thickly sliced
½ small melon,
    peeled, seeded and cubed
½ small pineapple,
    peeled and cubed, or
    × 225 g/8 oz can pineapple
    cubes, drained
TO GARNISH:
flaked almonds, toasted
chopped fresh parsley

1. Put the coconut into a small bowl and pour in the boiling water. Set aside.
2. Melt the butter in a flameproof casserole, add the onions and cook gently until soft and golden. Mix in the curry paste and flour and cook for 2 minutes.
3. Strain the 'milk' from the coconut and stir into the casserole with the stock, apricot jam and lemon juice. Season to taste with salt and pepper.
4. Bring to the boil, then cover and cook in a preheated oven for 25 minutes.
5. Add the fruit to the casserole and mix well. Adjust the seasoning, re-cover and cook for a further 20 minutes.
6. Garnish with almonds and parsley, and serve with a herb and nut rice and/or a chicken curry.

MIXED VEGETABLE CURRY S

Preparation time: 15 minutes
Cooking time: Low 7-9 hours
*   High 3-4 hours*

2 tablespoons vegetable oil
1 large onion,
    peeled and chopped
450 g/1 lb potatoes, peeled and
    cut into 1 cm/½ inch cubes
3 carrots, scraped and sliced
2 celery sticks, cut into 1 cm/
    ½ inch pieces
1 green pepper,
    cored, seeded and chopped
1 tablespoon curry powder
1 tablespoon tomato purée
1 tablespoon lemon juice
300 ml/½ pint hot chicken stock
salt
2 hard-boiled eggs, quartered,
    to garnish

1. Heat the oil in a frying pan. Add the onion and fry until transparent. Stir in the potatoes and fry until they are beginning to colour. Transfer both to the stoneware pot.
2. Add the carrots, celery and green pepper to the frying pan and fry until lightly browned. Transfer to the stoneware pot.
3. Stir the curry powder, tomato purée and lemon juice into the residues left in the frying pan. Fry for 1 minute, stirring. Gradually stir in the stock and a little salt and bring to the boil. Pour over the vegetables in the stoneware pot.
4. Cover and cook on Low for 6-8 hours or High for 3-4 hours. If possible, stir once during cooking.
5. Stir well and taste and adjust the seasoning. Serve garnished with the hard-boiled egg quarters, as a main course.

Top: Curried fruit casserole
Bottom: Mixed vegetable curry

MARROW MADRAS S

Preparation time: 10 minutes
Cooking time: Low 6-8 hours
*   High 3-4 hours*

1 tablespoon oil
1 small onion,
   peeled and finely chopped
1 small dessert apple,
   peeled, cored and chopped
225 g/8 oz minced beef
2 teaspoons curry powder
2 teaspoons plain flour
1 tablespoon tomato purée
salt
1 medium marrow, peeled,
   halved lengthways and
   seeded
300 ml/½ pint hot beef stock

1. Heat the oil in a frying pan. Add the onion and apple and fry until the onion is transparent. Add the minced beef and continue frying until the beef is evenly browned.
2. Stir in the curry powder, flour and tomato purée. Cook until all the liquid has evaporated. Season lightly with salt.
3. Divide the beef mixture between the marrow halves and press it in firmly.
4. Stand the stuffed marrow halves in the stoneware pot and pour the hot stock around them.
5. Cover and cook on Low for 6-8 hours or High for 3-4 hours. Serve as a supper dish.

VEGETABLE CASSEROLE WITH CHEESE DUMPLINGS P

Preparation time: 15 minutes
Cooking time: H pressure 3 minutes
*   Simmering 10 minutes*

2 medium onions,
   peeled and chopped
6 carrots, scraped and sliced
6 celery sticks, finely chopped
1 medium parsnip, peeled and
   cut into 1 cm/½ inch cubes
1 small swede, peeled and
   cut into 1 cm/½ inch cubes
450 ml/¾ pint beef stock
1 tablespoon tomato purée
½ teaspoon dried mixed herbs
salt
freshly ground black pepper
DUMPLINGS:
100 g/4 oz self-raising flour
½ teaspoon salt
50 g/2 oz shredded beef suet
50 g/2 oz Cheddar cheese,
   finely grated
about 4 tablespoons water
TO SERVE:
1 tablespoon finely grated
   Cheddar cheese
1 tablespoon chopped fresh
   parsley

1. Put all the vegetables, the stock, tomato purée, herbs and salt and pepper to taste into the cooker. Stir well.
2. Close the cooker, bring to H pressure and cook for 3 minutes.
3. Meanwhile, prepare the dumplings. Sift the flour and salt into a bowl and stir in the suet and cheese. Add as much of the water as necessary to mix to a firm dough that leaves the sides of the bowl cleanly. Divide into eight pieces and form into balls.
4. Reduce the pressure of the cooker quickly. Add the dumplings to the vegetables. Cover the cooker but do not close it fully, and remove the weights.
5. Simmer gently for 10 minutes or until the dumplings are well risen and cooked.
6. Serve sprinkled with cheese and parsley, as a main meal.

Top: Marrow Madras
Bottom: Vegetable casserole with cheese dumplings

MIXED BEAN CASSEROLE [P]

Preparation time: 6 minutes,
  plus soaking time
Cooking time: H pressure 20 minutes

100 g/4 oz dried red kidney beans
100 g/4 oz dried white haricot
  beans
100 g/4 oz dried chick peas
1 litre/2 pints boiling water
1 tablespoon vegetable oil
1 large onion,
  peeled and chopped
1 green pepper,
  cored, seeded and chopped
3 tablespoons tomato purée
750 ml/1¼ pints beef stock
2 tablespoons demerara sugar
1 teaspoon dry mustard
freshly ground black pepper
salt
chopped fresh parsley, to garnish

When cooked the chick peas will not be as soft as the kidney or haricot beans. This gives an interesting texture to the recipe.

1. Put all the beans in a large bowl. Cover with the boiling water and leave to soak for 1 hour. Drain well.
2. Heat the oil in the open cooker. Add the onion and green pepper and fry until the onion is transparent.
3. Add the beans with the tomato purée, stock, sugar, mustard and pepper to taste and stir well.
4. Close the cooker, bring to H pressure and cook for 20 minutes. Reduce the pressure slowly.
5. Taste and adjust the seasoning, adding a little salt. Sprinkle with parsley before serving as an accompanying vegetable.

BUTTER BEANS BRETON

Preparation time: 20 minutes,
  plus soaking time
Cooking time: 1½-2 hours
Oven: 180℃, 350 °F, Gas Mark 4

50 g/2 oz butter
2 onions,
  peeled and finely chopped
225 g/8 oz dried butter beans,
  soaked in water overnight
  and drained
2 sprigs fresh savory, or
  1 teaspoon dried savory
600 ml/1 pint chicken or
  vegetable stock
1 teaspoon ground nutmeg
salt
freshly ground black pepper
150 ml/¼ pint double cream
cooked green beans, to garnish

1. Melt the butter in a flameproof casserole, add the onions and cook until softened. Stir in the beans.
2. Mix in the savory, stock and nutmeg and season to taste with salt and pepper. Cover the casserole and transfer to a preheated oven. Cook for 1½ hours or until the beans are tender and the stock has been absorbed.
3. Stir in the cream, adjust the seasoning, cover and return to the oven for 10 minutes.
4. Garnish with green beans and serve with pork or bacon dishes.

Above left: Mixed bean casserole
Above right: Butter beans Breton

Right: Risotto

RISOTTO P

Preparation time: 9 minutes
Cooking time: H pressure 5 minutes

1 tablespoon vegetable oil
1 medium onion,
    peeled and chopped
1 garlic clove, crushed
1 green or red pepper,
    cored, seeded and chopped
50 g/2 oz mushrooms, chopped
275 g/10 oz long-grain rice
750 ml/1¼ pints chicken stock
100 g/4 oz sweetcorn kernels
    (thawed if frozen)
½ teaspoon grated nutmeg
salt
freshly ground black pepper
1 tablespoon chopped chives or
    spring onions

1. Heat the oil in the open cooker. Add the onion, garlic and green or red pepper and fry until all are beginning to soften.
2. Stir in the mushrooms and rice and continue frying for a few moments to absorb any excess oil.
3. Add the stock, sweetcorn, nutmeg and salt and pepper to taste and stir well.
4. Close the cooker, bring to H pressure and cook for 5 minutes. Reduce the pressure quickly.
5. Stir the risotto well; if there is any excess liquid, put the open cooker back on a low heat and cook for a few minutes until it has evaporated. Taste and adjust the seasoning.
6. Serve as a supper dish, sprinkled with the chives or spring onions.

ITALIAN VEGETABLES

P

Preparation time: 20 minutes
Cooking time: H pressure 3 minutes

2 tablespoons vegetable oil
1 medium onion,
    peeled and chopped
1 garlic clove, peeled and crushed
4 courgettes,
    cut into 2.5 cm/1 inch pieces
1 small cauliflower,
    divided into large florets
4 tomatoes,
    skinned and quartered
150 ml/¼ pint chicken stock
½ teaspoon dried oregano
salt
freshly ground black pepper

1. Heat the oil in the open cooker. Add the onion, garlic and courgettes and fry until they are lightly browned. Drain off any excess oil.
2. Add the cauliflower, tomatoes, stock, herbs and salt and pepper to taste and stir well.
3. Close the cooker, bring to H pressure and cook for 3 minutes. Reduce the pressure quickly.
4. Carefully lift out the vegetables and keep hot on a warmed serving dish.

Return the open cooker to the heat and boil the liquid rapidly for several minutes to reduce it. Taste and adjust the seasoning, then pour over the vegetables. Serve as an accompanying dish to a main meal.

Below left: Italian vegetables
Below right: Aubergine layer
Bottom left: Greek-style peppers
Bottom right: Tomato and courgette casserole

AUBERGINE LAYER

Preparation time: 30 minutes
Cooking time: 1 hour
Oven: 180°C, 350°F, Gas Mark 4

2 medium aubergines, trimmed
salt
4 tablespoons oil
2 onions, peeled and sliced
4 tomatoes, skinned and sliced
50 g/2 oz walnuts,
    coarsely chopped
300 ml/½ pint tomato juice
freshly ground black pepper
1 teaspoon chopped fresh basil or
    ½ teaspoon dried basil
50 g/2 oz Seasoned Crumbs,
    (page 140)

1. Slice the aubergine, sprinkle with salt and leave for 30 minutes. Rinse well under cold water and pat dry with kitchen paper.
2. Heat 3 tablespoons of the oil in a large frying pan, fry the aubergines on each side until lightly coloured and reserve. Add the remaining oil to the pan and cook the onions gently until soft and golden. Reserve.
3. Layer the aubergines, onions, tomatoes and walnuts in a casserole. Season the tomato juice with salt and pepper, add the basil and pour over the vegetables. Cover and cook in a preheated oven for 45 minutes.
4. Sprinkle with the breadcrumbs and return, uncovered, to the oven for 15 minutes until golden and bubbling.
5. Serve with braised brown rice and a salad including watercress and chicory.

TOMATO & COURGETTE CASSEROLE

S

Serves 4-6
Preparation time: 15 minutes
Cooking time: Low 6-8 hours
*   High 3-4 hours*

450 g/1 lb courgettes,
    thinly sliced
450 g/1 lb fim tomatoes,
    skinned and thickly sliced
1 small onion, peeled and grated
½ teaspoon dried basil
salt
freshly ground black pepper
2 tablespoons water

If this recipe is cooked on the high setting you will need twice the amount of water.

1. Spread half the courgettes over the bottom of the stoneware pot. Cover with half the tomatoes and sprinkle with half of the onion and basil and salt and pepper.
2. Repeat these layers again and add the water.
3. Cover and cook on Low for 6-8 hours or High for 3-4 hours. Taste and adjust the seasoning before serving.

GREEK-STYLE PEPPERS

S

Preparation time: 20 minutes
Cooking time: Low 6-8 hours
*   High 3-4 hours*

75 g/3 oz long-grain rice
4 medium green peppers
1 garlic clove,
     peeled and crushed
350 g/12 oz cooked lamb,
     finely chopped
50 g/2 oz sultanas
salt
freshly ground black pepper
1 × 400 g/14 oz can tomatoes,
     chopped, with their juice

1. Cook the rice in boiling salted water in a saucepan for about 10 minutes or until tender. Drain in a sieve, if necessary, and rinse with boiling water.
2. Carefully cut a hole around the stalk end of each pepper and remove the core and seeds. If necessary, cut a thin slice from the base of each pepper so that it will stand upright.
3. Mix together the cooked rice, garlic, lamb, sultanas and a little salt and pepper.

4. Pack the stuffing into the peppers, pressing it down well.
5. Stand the peppers in the stoneware pot and pour the tomatoes around them.
6. Cover and cook on Low for 6-8 hours or High for 3-4 hours. Serve as a supper dish.

SPICED CABBAGE [P]

Preparation time: 7 minutes
Cooking time: H pressure 4 minutes

25 g/1 oz butter or margarine
1 firm medium green cabbage,
quartered and cored
½ teaspoon grated nutmeg
1 × 225 g/8 oz can tomatoes,
chopped, with their juice
2 tablespoons demerara sugar
4 tablespoons water
salt
freshly ground black pepper

1. Melt the butter or margarine in the open cooker. Add the cabbage quarters and carefully brown the cut surfaces. Add the remaining ingredients with salt and pepper to taste.
2. Close the cooker, bring to H pressure and cook for 4 minutes. Reduce the pressure quickly.
3. Lift out the cabbage quarters and keep hot on a warmed serving dish. Return the open cooker to the heat and boil the sauce rapidly for 2 minutes. Taste and adjust the seasoning, then pour it over the cabbage.

CASSEROLE OF CHESTNUTS, APPLE & PRUNES

Preparation time: 15 minutes,
plus soaking prunes and
cooking chestnuts
Cooking time: 1 hour
Oven: 180°C, 350°F, Gas Mark 4

25 g/1 oz butter
1 onion, peeled and chopped
225 g/8 oz prunes, soaked in
water overnight, drained and
pitted
225 g/8 oz chestnuts,
peeled and cooked
1 large cooking apple,
peeled, cored and sliced
1 tablespoon soft brown sugar
300 ml/½ pint dry red wine
1 stick cinnamon
salt
freshly ground black pepper
crisply fried bacon, crumbled,
to garnish

1. Melt the butter in a flameproof casserole, add the onion and cook until softened.
2. Stir in the prunes, chestnuts, apple, brown sugar, red wine and cinnamon. Season to taste with salt and pepper.
3. Bring to the boil, then cover and transfer to a preheated oven. Cook for 1 hour. Discard the cinnamon stick. Adjust the seasoning.
4. Garnish with bacon and serve with duck or game dishes.

CARROT & WALNUT BAKE

Preparation time: 10 minutes
Cooking time: 1 hour
Oven: 180°C, 350°F, Gas Mark 4

225 g/8 oz carrots,
   scraped, cooked and diced
225 g/8 oz frozen peas, thawed
50 g/2 oz walnuts, chopped
1 onion,
   peeled and finely chopped
50 g/2 oz fresh brown
   breadcrumbs
250 ml/8 fl oz milk
15 g/½ oz butter, melted
2 eggs, beaten
1 tablespoon creamed
   horseradish
salt
freshly ground black pepper
TO GARNISH:
cucumber twists
sliced stuffed olives

1. Mix together all the ingredients and season to taste with salt and pepper.
2. Pour into a greased casserole, cover and cook in a preheated oven for 1 hour.
3. Garnish with cucumber twists and sliced stuffed olives. Serve with tomato sauce, see Roman Pie (page 120).

Above left: Spiced cabbage
Above right: Casserole of chestnuts, apple and prunes

Left: Carrot and walnut bake

HAM & POTATO ST GERMAIN

Preparation time: 20 minutes
Cooking time: 1 hour
Oven: 160°C, 325°F, Gas Mark 3

100 g/4 oz bacon, rind removed,
   diced
25 g/1 oz butter
8 button onions, peeled
25 g/1 oz plain flour
450 ml/¾ pint ham, vegetable or
   chicken stock
pinch of sugar
1 teaspoon chopped fresh mint
salt
freshly ground black pepper
2 potatoes, peeled and diced
450 g/1 lb green peas,
   fresh or frozen
sprig of fresh mint, to garnish

1. Cook the bacon in a dry frying pan until the fat runs. Transfer to a casserole.
2. Add the butter to the bacon fat, gently fry the onions until golden, and add to the casserole. Stir the flour into the fat, and cook for 2 minutes.
3. Blend in the stock, stirring, bring to the boil and add the sugar and mint.
4. Season with salt and pepper, and pour into the casserole. Add the potatoes. Mix, cover, and cook in a preheated oven for 40 minutes.
5. Carefully stir in the peas. Cover, and return to the oven for 20 minutes or until the peas are tender. (Fresh ones will take longer than frozen peas.)
6. Garnish with fresh mint and serve with sausages or gammon.

POMMES SAVOYARDE

Preparation time: 20 minutes
Cooking time: about 1 hour
Oven: 180°C, 350°F, Gas Mark 4

50 g/2 oz butter
600 ml/1 pint vegetable or
   chicken stock
75 g/3 oz Gruyère cheese, grated
1 garlic clove,
   peeled and crushed
½ teaspoon ground nutmeg
750 g/1½ lb potatoes,
   peeled and thinly sliced
salt
freshly ground black pepper
chopped fresh parsley,
   to garnish

1. Grease a casserole with 25 g/1 oz of the butter.
2. Mix together the stock, 50 g/2 oz of the cheese, the garlic and nutmeg. Fold in the potatoes. Season to taste with salt and pepper.
3. Pour into the casserole, cover and cook in a preheated oven for 50 minutes or until the potatoes are tender and the stock is reduced.
4. Sprinkle with the remaining cheese and dot with the rest of the butter. Return to the oven, uncovered, and cook for a further 15 minutes or until golden and bubbling.
5. Sprinkle with parsley, and serve with meat or fish dishes.

VEGETABLE CHOP SUEY   **P**

Preparation time: 8 minutes
Cooking time: H pressure 4 minutes

2 tablespoons vegetable oil
1 medium onion,
   peeled and chopped
3 celery sticks, finely chopped
1 red pepper,
   cored, seeded and sliced
100 g/4 oz bean sprouts
100 g/4 oz mushrooms,
   thickly sliced
1 tablespoon soy sauce
300 ml/½ pint chicken stock
salt
freshly ground black pepper
2 teaspoons cornflour
1 tablespoon cold water

1. Heat the oil in the open cooker. Add the onion, celery and red pepper and fry gently until the onion is transparent. Drain off any excess oil.
2. Add the bean sprouts, mushrooms, soy sauce, stock and salt and pepper to taste to the cooker and stir well.
3. Close the cooker, bring to H pressure and cook for 4 minutes. Reduce the pressure quickly.
4. Return the cooker to the heat. Dissolve the cornflour in the cold water, add to the cooker and bring to the boil, stirring. Simmer until thickened. Taste and adjust the seasoning.
5. Serve with grilled chops or steaks.

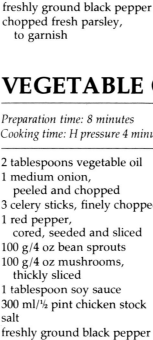

PAPRIKA POTATOES

Preparation time: 20 minutes
Cooking time: about 1 hour
Oven: 180°C, 350°F, Gas Mark 4

1 tablespoon oil
2 onions, peeled and sliced
1 tablespoon sweet paprika
1 garlic clove,
    peeled and crushed
300 ml/½ pint beef stock or
    1 × 275 g/10 oz can
    consommé
750 g/1½ lb potatoes,
    peeled and diced
2 tomatoes,
    skinned, seeded and diced
salt
freshly ground black pepper
4 tablespoons soured cream
    (optional)
thin green pepper rings,
    to garnish

1. Heat the oil in a flameproof casserole and cook the onions until soft. Stir in the paprika, garlic, stock or consommé, potatoes and tomatoes. Season with salt and pepper.
2. Bring to the simmer, cover and cook in a preheated oven for 1 hour or until the potatoes are tender and the stock is reduced. Stir in the soured cream.
3. Garnish with green pepper and serve with veal or pork dishes.

Top left: Green beans provençale
Top right: Vegetable scallop
Right: Scalloped beetroot

Below: Paprika potatoes

GREEN BEANS PROVENÇALE   P

Preparation time: 15 minutes
Cooking time: H pressure 3 minutes

1 tablespoon olive oil
1 small onion,
    peeled and chopped
1 garlic clove,
    peeled and crushed
750 g/1½ lb runner or French
    beans, trimmed and cut into
    5 cm/2 inch lengths
1 × 225 g/8 oz can tomatoes
2 tablespoons white wine
salt
freshly ground black pepper
chopped fresh parsley,
    to garnish

1. Heat the oil in the open cooker. Add the onion, garlic and beans and fry gently for 2-3 minutes.
2. Add the tomatoes with their juice, the wine and salt and pepper to taste.
3. Close the cooker, bring to H pressure and cook for 3 minutes. Reduce the pressure quickly.
4. Taste and adjust the seasoning, and serve sprinkled with parsley.

VEGETABLE SCALLOP

Preparation time: 20 minutes
Cooking time: 40 minutes
Oven: 180°C, 350°F, Gas Mark 4

225 g/8 oz peas
225 g/8 oz sweetcorn
100 g/4 oz mushrooms, sliced
pinch of sugar
300 ml/½ pint hot Parsley Sauce
    (page 81)
½ teaspoon ground nutmeg
salt
freshly ground black pepper
3 tomatoes, skinned and sliced
50 g/2 oz Seasoned Crumbs
    (page 140)
sprig of fresh mint, to garnish

Fresh, frozen or canned peas and sweetcorn kernels may be used.

1. Mix together the peas, sweetcorn, mushrooms and sugar. Stir in the parsley sauce and nutmeg, and season to taste with salt and pepper.
2. Pour into a shallow casserole, cover and cook in a preheated oven for 30 minutes.
3. Lay the tomato slices over the top and sprinkle with the seasoned crumbs.
4. Return to the oven, uncovered, and continue cooking for 10 minutes or until golden.
5. Garnish with mint and serve with a cheese and potato pie.

SCALLOPED BEETROOT

Preparation time: 15 minutes
Cooking time: 45 minutes
Oven: 180℃, 350°F, Gas Mark 4

25 g/1 oz butter
25 g/1 oz plain flour
300 ml/½ pint clear strong beef
    stock or canned consommé
2 tablespoons cider vinegar
1 teaspoon sugar
salt
freshly ground black pepper
450 g/1 lb cooked beetroot,
    skinned and sliced
4 streaky bacon rashers,
    rind removed
TO GARNISH:
watercress
soured cream

1. Melt the butter in a saucepan, stir in the flour and cook for 2 minutes.
2. Gradually stir in the stock or consommé, cider vinegar and sugar, bring to the boil, and season with salt and pepper.
3. Put the beetroot into the casserole and pour the sauce over the beetroot. Cover and cook in a preheated oven for 30 minutes.
4. Twist the bacon rashers, and place them on top of the beetroot. Return to the oven, uncover, for 15 minutes until the bacon is crisp.
5. Garnish with watercress and top each serving with a spoonful of soured cream. Serve with grilled pork sausages.

PARTY CASSEROLES

GINGERED GAMMON ⬛**P**

Serves 6 to 8
Preparation time: 5 minutes
Cooking time: H pressure 24 minutes
Oven: 15 minutes (200°C, 400°F, Gas Mark 6)

1½ kg/3 lb piece of middle or
   corner gammon
900 ml/1½ pints ginger beer
2 bay leaves
TO FINISH:
1 teaspoon ground ginger
2 tablespoons clear honey
few whole cloves

1. Place the gammon in the cooker and add sufficient cold water to cover. Bring to the boil in the open pan, then drain and discard the water.
2. Add the ginger beer to the cooker with the bay leaves.
3. Close the cooker, bring to H pressure and cook for 24 minutes. Reduce the pressure quickly.
4. Lift out the gammon and cool for a few minutes before carefully removing the brown outer skin. Score the fat into a diamond pattern. Place the gammon in a roasting tin.
5. Mix together the ground ginger and honey and spread half of the mixture over the gammon. Spike the fat with a few whole cloves.
6. Bake at the top of a moderately hot oven for 5 minutes. Pour over the remaining ginger glaze and continue baking for a further 10 minutes.
7. Serve cold, in slices, with mixed salads.

TURKEY AMANDINE

Serves 8
Preparation time: 30 minutes,
*   plus chilling time*
Cooking time: 1 hour
Oven: 160°C, 325°F, Gas Mark 3

1 × 1¼ kg/2½ lb turkey breast
600 ml/1 pint turkey or chicken
   stock
1 onion, peeled and stuck with
   1 clove
450 ml/¾ pint mayonnaise
150 ml/¼ pint soured cream
6 spring onions, thinly sliced
75 g/3 oz blanched almonds,
   slivered
1 teaspoon chopped fresh
   tarragon, or ½ teaspoon dried
   tarragon
salt
freshly ground black pepper
TO GARNISH:
small lettuce leaves
canned pitted Morello cherries
French dressing

1. Place the turkey breast in a casserole, pour in the stock and add the onion. Cover and cook in a preheated oven for 1 hour.
2. Remove the lid and leave the turkey to cool in the stock.
3. Mix together the mayonnaise, soured cream, spring onions, almonds and tarragon. Season to taste with salt and pepper. The sauce should be a coating consistency; if it is too thick, thin it with a little of the stock.
4. Lift the turkey breast on to a board and carve into thin slices. Arrange on a serving dish and coat with the sauce.
5. Garnish with the lettuce leaves topped with cherries tossed in French dressing. Serve chilled.

CONTINENTAL BEAN SALAD　P

Serves 8
Preparation time: 10 minutes,
*   plus soaking time*
Cooking time: H pressure 15 minutes

175 g/6 oz dried haricot beans
175 g/6 oz dried red kidney
   beans
900 ml/1½ pints cold water
1 medium onion,
   peeled and finely chopped
1 small green pepper, cored,
   seeded and finely chopped
100 g/4 oz garlic sausage or
   salami, cut into 1 cm/½ inch
   cubes
3 tablespoons olive oil
1 tablespoon wine vinegar
pinch of dried mixed herbs
16 stuffed green olives
salt
freshly ground black pepper

1. Put the beans into a large bowl, cover with boiling water and leave to soak for 1 hour. Drain and discard the water.
2. Transfer the beans to the cooker and add the cold water.
3. Close the cooker, bring to H pressure and cook for 15 minutes. Reduce the pressure slowly.
4. Drain the beans in a colander. Transfer them to a serving dish and stir in all the remaining ingredients with salt and pepper to taste. (If this dish is being made in advance do not add the oil and vinegar until just before serving.)

Right: Continental bean salad
Far right: Mushrooms à la grecque

TURKEY TERRINE

Serves 10
Preparation time: 45 minutes,
  plus marinating time
Cooking time: 1½ hours
Oven: 180°C, 350°F, Gas Mark 4

Below left: Turkey amandine
Below right: Turkey terrine

1 kg/2 lb cooked boneless
  turkey
150 ml/¼ pint brandy
salt
freshly ground black pepper
50 g/2 oz butter
450 g/1 lb chicken livers,
  trimmed
225 g/8 oz salt pork
1 onion, peeled
2 garlic cloves,
  peeled and crushed
2 sprigs fresh parsley
3 tablespoons milk
1 thick slice of bread,
  crust removed
1 egg, beaten
pinch of mixed spice
1 teaspoon tomato purée
450 g/1 lb streaky bacon,
  rind removed
1 bay leaf
TO GARNISH:
watercress
chopped walnuts

This terrine can be served direct from the casserole, or turned out.

1. Slice 450 g/1 lb of the turkey into matchstick-sized pieces and put into a bowl. Pour over the brandy and season lightly. Leave for several hours, stirring occasionally.
2. Melt the butter in a frying pan and cook the livers briskly for 3-4 minutes. Drain, slice and reserve.
3. Pass through the mincer the remaining 450 g/1 lb of turkey, the pork, onion, garlic and parsley.
4. Soak the bread in the milk for a few minutes. Squeeze as dry as possible and mix with the minced ingredients.
5. Add the egg, spice and tomato purée, and season with pepper only. Strain the turkey strips and reserve the brandy.
6. Line the bottom and sides of a casserole with about three-quarters of the bacon rashers, and the strips of liver.
7. Layer the minced ingredients and turkey strips, finishing with the mince.
8. Using a skewer, pierce a few holes in the mixture and pour in the reserved brandy. Leave for a few minutes, then press the contents well down in the dish.
9. Cover with the remaining bacon and top with the bay leaf. Cover closely with foil, then the casserole lid. Place the casserole in a roasting tin half filled with hot water and cook in a preheated oven for 1½ hours. Leave until cold.
10. Invert on to a board and remove the surplus fat, then turn back on to a serving dish. Garnish with watercress and walnuts and serve with potato salad.

MUSHROOMS A LA GRECQUE $\boxed{\text{S}}$

Serves 8
Preparation time: 15 minutes
Cooking time: Low 3-4 hours
  High 1½-2 hours

750 g/1½ lb button mushrooms,
  cleaned
1 large onion,
  peeled and finely chopped
1 garlic clove,
  peeled and crushed
6 tablespoons tomato purée
3 tablespoons wine vinegar
300 ml/½ pint water
4 tablespoons vegetable or olive
  oil
salt
freshly ground black pepper
chopped fresh parsley, to garnish

1. Put all the ingredients except the parsley into the stoneware pot and stir well.
2. Cover and cook on Low for 3-4 hours or High for 1½-2 hours.
3. Stir well, and taste and adjust the seasoning. Sprinkle with the parsley and serve hot or cold.

HOT FISH DIP   S

Serves about 12
Preparation time: 5 minutes
Cooking time: High 1½ hours

2 × 400 g/14 oz cans lobster or
  prawn bisque
1 × 212 g/7½ oz can crab meat,
  drained and flaked
100 g/4 oz cooked peeled
  prawns, chopped
¼ teaspoon dried basil
salt
freshly ground black pepper

1. Put all the ingredients, with salt and pepper to taste, into the stoneware pot and stir well.
2. Cover and cook on High for 1½ hours.
3. Stir well, then turn to Low to keep hot while serving. Serve with chunks of French bread or fingers of hot toast, as part of a buffet.

CURRIED FISH RING   P

Serves 6
Preparation time: 20 minutes,
  plus chilling
Cooking time: H pressure 5 minutes

750 ml/1¼ pints water
350 g/12 oz cod fillets
salt
freshly ground black pepper
225 g/8 oz long-grain rice
1 small onion,
  peeled and grated
1 small green pepper,
  cored, seeded and finely
  chopped
good pinch of powdered saffron
TO FINISH:
4 tablespoons mayonnaise
1 teaspoon curry paste
pinch of chilli powder
100 g/4 oz shelled prawns
1 lemon, thinly sliced

1. Put 300 ml/½ pint of the water in the cooker and add the trivet, rim side down.
2. Lightly grease a large piece of foil. Lay the cod on the foil and add salt and pepper. Fold the foil into a parcel around the fish. Place the parcel on the trivet.
3. If using a perforated separator, line it with a piece of foil; otherwise use a heatproof container that will fit easily into the cooker. Put the rice, onion, green pepper, saffron, remaining water and a little salt into the container. Place the container on top of the fish parcel.
4. Close the cooker, bring to H pressure and cook for 5 minutes. Reduce the pressure slowly.
5. Lift out the container and transfer the rice mixture into a greased 1 litre/2 pint ring mould. Press down firmly and leave to chill thoroughly.
6. Remove the skin from the fish and cut it into small chunks. Chill.
7. Mix together the mayonnaise, curry paste and chilli powder. Carefully fold in the fish and prawns, reserving a few prawns to use for garnishing.
8. When the rice ring is firm and cold, turn it out on to a flat plate. Fill the centre with the curried fish mixture and garnish with the remaining prawns and twists of lemon.

Top left: Hot fish dip
Top right: Prawn gumbo with rice
Bottom left: Curried fish ring
Bottom right: Seafood chowder

PRAWN GUMBO WITH RICE

Serves 8
Preparation time: 30 minutes
Cooking time: 1¼ hours
Oven: 160°C, 325°F, Gas Mark 3

2 tablespoons oil
2 sticks celery, finely sliced
1 onion, peeled and diced
1 green pepper,
    seeded and diced
1 garlic clove,
    peeled and crushed
1 tablespoon Worcestershire
    sauce
1 × 425 g/15 oz can tomatoes
300 ml/½ pint tomato juice
salt
freshly ground black pepper
100 g/4 oz long-grain rice
100 g/4 oz okra,
    stem removed, sliced
225 g/8 oz peeled prawns,
    fresh or frozen
225 g/8 oz dressed crab meat,
    fresh or frozen
4 tablespoons dry sherry
TO GARNISH:
Garlic Croûtons (page 141)
chopped fresh parsley

1. Heat the oil in a flameproof casserole, cook the celery, onion and pepper gently for 5 minutes.
2. Add the garlic, Worcestershire sauce, tomatoes, tomato juice, and season with salt and pepper.
3. Stir in the rice and okra, and bring gently to simmering point. Cover, and cook in a preheated oven for 1 hour.
4. Gently stir in the prawns, crab meat and sherry (if the rice looks a little dry, add a little more tomato juice).
5. Re-cover, and return to the oven for 15 minutes. Pour into a heated serving dish, group the croûtons at either end and sprinkle with parsley.

SEAFOOD CHOWDER   P

Serves 8 to 10
Preparation time: 20 minutes
Cooking time: H pressure 3 minutes

1 tablespoon vegetable oil
2 medium onions,
    peeled and chopped
225 g/8 oz unsmoked bacon
    rashers, rind removed,
    chopped
350 g/12 oz cod fillet, skinned
    and cut into 2.5 cm/1 inch
    pieces
350 g/12 oz haddock fillet,
    skinned and cut into 2.5 cm/
    1 inch pieces
100 g/4 oz sweetcorn kernels
450 g/1 lb potatoes, peeled and
    cut into 1 cm/½ inch cubes
100 g/4 oz cooked shelled
    prawns
900 ml/1½ pints chicken stock
    or water
2 tablespoons tomato purée
1 teaspoon dried basil
salt
freshly ground black pepper
1 tablespoon cornflour
1½ tablespoons cold water
chopped fresh parsley, to garnish

1. Heat the oil in the open cooker. Add the onion and bacon and fry until both are beginning to brown. Drain off any excess oil.
2. Add the remaining ingredients, except the cornflour, water and parsley, to the cooker and stir well.
3. Close the cooker, bring to H pressure and cook for 3 minutes. Reduce the pressure quickly.
4. Return the open cooker to the heat. Dissolve the cornflour in the cold water and stir into the chowder. Bring to the boil, stirring carefully, and simmer until thickened. Taste and adjust the seasoning.
5. Pour into a warmed tureen and sprinkle with the parsley. Serve with thick slices of hot French bread.

SWEET SOUR PORK & BEAN BAKE

Serves 12
Preparation time: 1 hour 20
  minutes,
    plus soaking time
Cooking time: 1½ hours
Oven 160°C, 325°F, Gas Mark 3

1 kg/2 lb dried butter beans,
  soaked in water overnight
  and drained
3 tablespoons oil
1 kg/2 lb boned pork shoulder,
  cubed
1 onion,
  peeled and finely chopped
300 ml/½ pint tomato ketchup
juice of 2 lemons
2 tablespoons Dijon mustard
2 teaspoons chopped fresh basil
  or 1 teaspoon dried basil
120 ml/4 fl oz white wine
  vinegar
2 tablespoons soft brown sugar
300 ml/½ pint hot chicken stock
salt
freshly ground black pepper

1. Put the beans into a saucepan, cover with fresh cold water and bring to the boil. Simmer for 1 hour, then drain.
2. Heat the oil in a large frying pan, add the pork and brown on all sides. Transfer to a deep casserole.
3. Add the onion to the pan and cook gently until softened. Add to the casserole together with the beans, ketchup, lemon juice, mustard, basil, vinegar, brown sugar and stock. Season to taste with salt and pepper and mix well.
4. Cover the casserole and cook in a preheated oven for 1½ hours or until the meat is tender and the sauce is the consistency of thick cream.
5. Adjust the seasoning, then turn into a heated serving dish.

Top: **Sweet sour pork and bean bake**
Above left: **Chinese pork ribs**
Above right: **Chinese spiced beef**

CHINESE PORK RIBS P

Serves 8
Preparation time: 10 minutes
Cooking time: H pressure 10 minutes

2 tablespoons vegetable oil
1 large onion, peeled and
  chopped
2 sheets pork belly ribs,
  chopped into single ribs
2 tablespoons demerara sugar
2 tablespoons malt vinegar
2 tablespoons soy sauce
2 tablespoons tomato purée
8 tablespoons orange juice
¼ teaspoon ground ginger
150 ml/¼ pint water
1 garlic clove,
  peeled and crushed
salt
2 teaspoons cornflour
TO GARNISH:
finely grated rind of 2 oranges
watercress

1. Heat the oil in the open cooker. Add the onion and fry until transparent. Lift out, draining well.
2. Add the pork ribs to the cooker, a few at a time, and brown evenly.
3. Mix together the sugar, vinegar, soy sauce, tomato purée, orange juice, ginger and all but 1 tablespoon of the water. Pour over the ribs in the cooker. Stir in the onion and garlic with a little salt.
4. Close the cooker, bring to H pressure and cook for 10 minutes. Reduce the pressure quickly.
5. Lift out the ribs and keep hot on a heated serving dish. Return the open cooker to the heat. Dissolve the cornflour in the reserved 1 tablespoon of water. Stir into the liquid in the cooker. Bring to the boil, stirring, and simmer until thickened. Taste and adjust the seasoning.
6. Pour the sauce over the ribs and garnish with the orange rind and watercress.

CHINESE SPICED BEEF

Serves 6
Preparation time: 20 minutes
Cooking time: 2 hours
Oven: 160°C, 325°F, Gas Mark 3
  180°C, 350°F, Gas Mark 4

2 tablespoons oil
1 × 1¼ kg/2½ lb joint beef
  topside
3 tablespoons soy sauce
3 slices fresh root ginger,
  peeled and crushed
2 pieces star anise
1 stick cinnamon
1 tablespoon soft brown sugar
2 garlic cloves,
  peeled and crushed
450 ml/¾ pint water
salt
3 tablespoons sherry
sprigs of watercress, to garnish

Star anise and fresh root ginger are available in shops and supermarkets with a foreign delicatessen department. Fresh root ginger is also frequently available in good greengrocers.

1. Heat the oil in a large flameproof casserole, add the beef and brown on all sides.
2. Add the soy sauce, ginger, anise, cinnamon, brown sugar, garlic and water. Stir in 1 teaspoon salt.
3. Bring very slowly to the boil, then cover and transfer to a preheated oven. Cook for 1½ hours.
4. Stir in the sherry, raise the oven temperature and continue cooking, uncovered, for 30 minutes, basting several times until the sauce is reduced.

5. Remove the beef, slice it thinly and arrange on a heated serving dish.
6. Strain the sauce into a saucepan and adjust the seasoning. Bring to the boil and pour it over the beef. Garnish with watercress.
7. Serve hot with boiled or fried rice and stir-fried Chinese cabbage, or cold with quartered hard-boiled eggs, shredded cooked ham and spring onions.

ROMAN PIE

Serves 12
Preparaton time: 1¾ hours
Cooking time: 1½ hours
Oven: 180°C, 350°F, Gas Mark 4

1¾ kg/4 lb potatoes, peeled

TOMATO SAUCE:
450 g/1 lb ripe tomatoes, sliced,
    or 1 × 425 g/15 oz can
    tomatoes, drained and
    chopped
1 small onion,
    peeled and chopped
1 garlic clove,
    peeled and crushed
½ teaspoon dried basil
pinch of sugar
2 streaky bacon rashers,
    rind removed, diced
salt
freshly ground black pepper

4 eggs, beaten
100 g/4 oz Parmesan cheese,
    grated
salt
freshly ground black pepper
4 tablespoons chopped fresh
    parsley
1 whole nutmeg, grated
1¾ kg/4 lb minced beef
4 garlic cloves,
    peeled and crushed
120 ml/4 fl oz cold water
50 g/2 oz seasoned flour
4 tablespoons oil
450 g/1 lb mature Cheddar
    cheese, grated

TO GARNISH:
sautéed sliced courgettes
very thin onion rings

1. Cook the potatoes in boiling water.
2. Meanwhile make the tomato sauce. Put the tomatoes, onion, garlic, basil, sugar and bacon in a saucepan and bring slowly to the boil. Cover and leave to simmer gently until the liquid is very much reduced and the sauce is thick.
3. Rub the tomato sauce through a sieve and season to taste with salt and pepper.
4. When the potatoes are tender drain them well, then tip into a mixing bowl and mash until smooth.
5. Beat in the eggs and Parmesan cheese. Season to taste with salt and pepper, then mix in the parsley and nutmeg. Cover and reserve.
6. Mix together the beef, garlic and cold water, working it thoroughly with a wet hand. Season well with salt and pepper. Form into small balls and coat them in the seasoned flour.
7. Heat the oil in a large frying pan, add the beef balls a few at a time and brown on all sides. Transfer to a plate.
8. Layer the potato, beef balls, tomato sauce and all but 100 g/4 oz of the Cheddar cheese into 2 large deep casseroles, finishing with potato. Cover the casseroles and cook in a preheated oven for 45 minutes.
9. Remove the lids and sprinkle each casserole with the reserved Cheddar cheese. Return to the oven, uncovered, and cook for a further 10-15 minutes or until golden brown.
10. Serve garnished with courgette slices and onion rings.
11. This is a very substantial dish to a green salad with plenty of fresh watercress is a good accompaniment.

MEXICAN MEATBALLS ⬜S

Serves 12
Preparation time: 40 minutes
Cooking time: Low 6-8 hours
*   High 3-4 hours*

1¼ kg/2½ lb lean minced beef
1 large onion, peeled and grated
1 garlic clove,
    peeled and crushed
1 teaspoon chilli powder
2 tablespoons plain flour
salt
1 egg (size 2), beaten
2 tablespoons oil
2 red or green peppers,
    cored, seeded and thinly
    sliced
300 ml/½ pint hot beef stock
1 teaspoon Tabasco sauce
2 tablespoons tomato purée
freshly ground black pepper

Chilli powder is very hot and varies in strength depending on the manufacturer, so it is wise to use it cautiously.

1. Mix together the minced beef, onion, garlic, chilli powder, flour and a little salt. Gradually mix in the egg to bind the ingredients.
2. Divide the mixture into 36 pieces on a floured surface. Form into balls.
3. Heat the oil in a frying pan. Add the meatballs, a few at a time, and brown on all sides. Transfer them to the stoneware pot.
4. Add the red or green peppers to the hot fat in the frying pan and fry lightly. Transfer to the stoneware pot, draining well.
5. Mix together the hot stock, Tabasco, tomato purée and a little salt and pepper. Pour over the other ingredients in the stoneware pot.
6. Cover and cook on Low for 6-8 hours or High for 3-4 hours.

ITALIAN BEEF CASSEROLE

Serves 10
Preparation time: 30 minutes
Cooking time: 1 hour
Oven: 180°C, 350°F, Gas Mark 4

100 g/4 oz butter
1 kg/2 lb beef topside, cut into
    5 mm/¼ inch dice
225 g/8 oz cooked ham, cut into
    5 mm/¼ inch dice
225 g/8 oz chicken livers, sliced
2 large onions, peeled and
    very finely chopped
2 carrots, scraped and very
    finely diced
3 sticks celery, very thinly sliced
2 teaspoons chopped fresh
    marjoram or 1 teaspoon dried
    marjoram
½ teaspoon ground cloves
2 tablespoons tomato purée
450 ml/¾ pint beef stock
salt
freshly ground black pepper
225 g/8 oz button mushrooms,
    quartered
300 ml/½ pint double cream
black olives, to garnish

1. Melt the butter in a large flameproof casserole, add the beef, ham and livers and brown lightly.
2. Stir in the vegetables and marjoram and cook over very gentle heat for 10 minutes.
3. Add the cloves, tomato purée and beef stock. Season carefully with salt and pepper and bring slowly to the boil.
4. Cover the casserole and transfer to a preheated oven. Cook for 40 minutes.
5. Stir in the mushrooms and cream. Adjust the seasoning. Re-cover and cook for a further 10 minutes.
6. Pour into a heated serving dish and garnish with black olives. Serve with hot buttered spaghetti or noodles.

Above: Mexican meatballs

Far left: Roman pie
Left: Italian beef casserole

CASSEROLE OF RED CABBAGE WITH AUSTRIAN SAUSAGE

Serves 8
Preparation time: 30 minutes
Cooking time: 1½-2 hours
Oven: 160°C, 325°F, Gas Mark 3

65 g/2½ oz butter
1 large onion, peeled and chopped
2 medium cooking apples, peeled, cored and diced
1 red cabbage, cored and finely shredded
finely grated rind and juice of 1 orange
3 tablespoons red wine vinegar
pinch of ground cloves
1 bay leaf
2 tablespoons soft brown sugar
150 ml/¼ pint dry red wine
150 ml/¼ pint beef stock
salt
freshly ground black pepper
1 kg/2 lb Vienna sausages
15 g/½ oz plain flour
TO GARNISH
1 dessert apple, cored, sliced and dipped in lemon juice
chopped fresh parsley

This dish can, with advantage, be made the previous day. It improves with keeping. Reheat carefully, and thicken just before serving.

1. Melt 50 g/2 oz of the butter in a large flameproof casserole, add the onion and cook gently until softened.
2. Stir in the apple, cabbage and orange rind and juice and toss well over the heat for 5 minutes.
3. Stir in the vinegar, cloves, bay leaf, soft brown sugar, red wine and stock and season to taste with salt and pepper. Bring slowly to the boil and remove from the heat.
4. Bury the sausages among the cabbage, cover the casserole and cook in a preheated oven for 1½-2 hours or until the cabbage is very tender.
5. Mix the remaining butter with the flour to make a paste and add to the cabbage. Place the casserole over heat on top of the stove and bring to the boil, stirring until the liquid has thickened.
6. Remove the bay leaf, then turn into a heated serving dish and garnish with apple slices and parsley.

AUTUMN HAM

Serves 8
Preparation time: 10 minutes
Cooking time: 1½-2 hours
Oven: 160°C, 325°F, Gas Mark 3

1 × 1.75 kg/4 lb gammon joint, rind removed
1 tablespoon whole cloves
1.2 litres/2 pints apple juice
2 sticks cinnamon
1 teaspoon whole allspice berries
1 tablespoon cornflour
salt
freshly ground black pepper
TO SERVE:
stewed sliced apples
chopped fresh sage

1. Stud the fat of the gammon joint with the cloves. Place in a casserole, pour in all but 2 tablespoons of the apple juice and add the cinnamon sticks and allspice. Cover and cook in a preheated oven for 1 hour.
2. Turn the joint over and continue cooking, covered, for 30 minutes to 1 hour or until tender.
3. Lift the gammon on to a board, slice and arrange on a heated serving dish. Keep hot.
4. Strain the cooking liquid into a saucepan. Dissolve the cornflour in the remaining apple juice, add to the pan and bring to the boil, stirring. Season if necessary with salt and pepper.
5. Pour the sauce over the gammon slices and serve with the stewed apples and sage. Baked potatoes and green salad make good accompaniments.

MOROCCAN LAMB S

Serves 8
Preparation time: 30 minutes
Cooking time: Low 8-10 hours
*　　　　　　High 4-5 hours*

---

2 tablespoons oil
1 large onion,
　peeled and thinly sliced
1 garlic clove,
　peeled and crushed
1½ kg/3 lb boned shoulder of
　lamb, cubed
1 × 400 g/14 oz can apricot
　halves
50 g/2 oz blanched almonds
½ teaspoon ground ginger
2 tablespoons tomato purée
300 ml/½ pint hot beef stock
salt
freshly ground black pepper
1 tablespoon cornflour
1½ tablespoons cold water

1. Heat the oil in a frying pan. Add the onion and garlic and fry until the onion is transparent. Transfer to the stoneware pot, draining well.
2. Add the lamb cubes to the frying pan and brown on all sides. Transfer to the stoneware pot. Drain the apricots, reserving the juice, and add to the pot with the almonds.
3. Mix together the reserved apricot juice, ginger, tomato purée and hot stock. Add to the pot with a little salt and pepper and stir well.
4. Cover and cook on Low for 8-10 hours or High for 4-5 hours.
5. Before serving, dissolve the cornflour in the cold water and stir into the lamb stew until thickened. Taste and adjust the seasoning.

Above left: Casserole of red cabbage with Austrian sausage
Above right: Autumn ham

Left: Moroccan lamb

CURRIED DRUMSTICKS

S

Serves 8
Preparation time: 20 minutes
Cooking time: Low 6-8 hours
  High 3-4 hours

25 g/1 oz butter
4 tablespoons vegetable oil
1 large onion,
  peeled and chopped
2 garlic cloves,
  peeled and crushed
1 large dessert apple,
  peeled, cored and chopped
16 chicken drumsticks
3 tablespoons mild curry
  powder
½ teaspoon chilli powder
3 tablespoons lemon juice
2 tablespoons tomato purée
450 ml/¾ pint hot chicken stock
100 g/4 oz sultanas
salt

Chilli powder is very hot and varies in strength depending on the manufacturer, so it is wise to use it cautiously.

1. Melt the butter with 2 tablespoons of the oil in a frying pan. Add the onion, garlic and apple and fry until the onion is transparent. Transfer to the stoneware pot, draining well.
2. Add the remaining oil to the frying pan. When it is hot, add the drumsticks, a few at a time, and brown on all sides.

Transfer to the stoneware pot.
3. Stir the curry and chilli powders into the residues in the frying pan and fry for a few moments before stirring in the lemon juice, tomato purée and stock. Bring to the boil, then pour into the stoneware pot. Add the sultanas and a little salt and stir well.
4. Cover and cook on Low for 6-8 hours or High for 3-4 hours.
5. Serve with plain boiled rice and curry accompaniments.

CHICKEN NORMANDY   [P]

Serves 8
Preparation time: 30 minutes
Cooking time: H pressure 6 minutes

50 g/2 oz butter
1 medium onion,
   peeled and chopped
2 garlic cloves,
   peeled and crushed
2 dessert apples,
   peeled, cored and chopped
16 large chicken drumsticks,
   skinned
4 tablespoons brandy
300 ml/½ pint chicken stock
salt
freshly ground black pepper
1 tablespoon cornflour
1½ tablespoons cold water
TO GARNISH:
50 g/2 oz butter
2 dessert apples,
   peeled, cored and cut into
   rings
4 tablespoons single cream
little paprika pepper

1. Melt the butter in the open cooker. Add the onion, garlic and apples and fry until the onion is transparent. Lift out, draining well.
2. Add the drumsticks to the cooker, a few at a time, and brown on all sides. When they are all browned, return them to the cooker with the onion, garlic and apples. Add the brandy, stock and salt and pepper to taste and stir well.
3. Close the cooker, bring to H pressure and cook for 6 minutes. Reduce the pressure quickly.
4. Lift out the drumsticks and keep hot on a heated serving dish. Mash the apples and onion into the cooking liquid and return the open pan to the heat. Dissolve the cornflour in the cold water and stir into the sauce. Bring to the boil, stirring, and simmer until thickened. Taste and adjust the seasoning, then pour over the chicken.
5. Rinse and dry the cooker. Melt the butter for the garnish in the open cooker. Add the apple rings and fry until they are golden brown. Drain on kitchen paper.
6. Pour the cream over the chicken, sprinkle with a little paprika pepper and garnish with the apple rings. Serve with boiled rice and a selection of salads.

MULLED WINE   [S]

Serves about 12
Preparation time: 10 minutes
Cooking time: High 1 hour

1 litre/2 pints red wine
300 ml/½ pint canned orange
   juice
4 tablespoons brown sugar
12 whole cloves
2 cinnamon sticks
1 orange, thinly sliced

1. Put all the ingredients, except the orange slices, in the stoneware pot and stir well.
2. Cover and heat on High for 1 hour.
3. Add the orange slices, and serve from the pot.

RUM FRUIT PUNCH   [S]

Serves about 12
Preparation time: 10 minutes
Cooking time: High 1 hour

2 lemons, thinly sliced
2 dessert apples,
   peeled, cored and chopped
2 tablespoons sugar
1 litre/2 pints red wine
300 ml/½ pint rum

1. Put the lemon slices, apples and sugar into the stoneware pot. Add the wine and rum and stir well.
2. Cover and heat on High for 1 hour. Serve hot.

Below left: Curried drumsticks
Centre left: Rum fruit punch
Bottom left: Mulled wine
Bottom right: Chicken Normandy

PUDDINGS

OLD-FASHIONED APPLE PUDDING Ⓟ

Preparation time: 25 minutes
Cooking time: steaming 15 minutes
*   L pressure 35 minutes*

100 g/4 oz self-raising flour
100 g/4 oz fresh white
    breadcrumbs
100 g/4 oz shredded suet
2 teaspoons caster sugar
about 150 ml/¼ pint cold water
450 g/1 lb cooking apples,
    peeled, cored and thinly
    sliced
50 g/2 oz sultanas
finely grated rind and juice of
    1 lemon
¼ teaspoon ground cinnamon
¼ teaspoon grated nutmeg
2 tablespoons demerara sugar
900 ml/1½ pints boiling water
little lemon juice or vinegar

1. Sift the flour into a mixing bowl. Stir in the breadcrumbs, suet and caster sugar. Gradually add enough of the cold water to make a smooth elastic dough that leaves the sides of the bowl clean.
2. Turn out the dough on to a floured surface and knead lightly. Take two-thirds of the dough and roll it out into a round large enough to line a greased 900 ml/1½ pint pudding basin.
3. Mix together the apples, sultanas, lemon rind and juice, cinnamon, nutmeg and demerara sugar. Pack into the basin, pressing down well.
4. Roll out the remaining dough to form a lid. Dampen the edges, place over the filling and press the edges together to seal.
5. Cover with a double thickness of greased greaseproof paper or a piece of greased foil and tie on securely.
6. Place the trivet in the cooker, rim side down, and pour in the boiling water and lemon juice or vinegar. Bring to the boil, then put the pudding on the trivet.
7. Close the cooker and steam gently for 15 minutes (without the weight). Raise the heat, bring to L pressure and cook for 35 minutes. Reduce the pressure slowly.
8. Turn out the pudding on to a heated serving dish and serve with hot custard.

BROWN BETTY

Preparation time: 20 minutes
Cooking time: 1 hour
Oven: 190°C, 375°F, Gas Mark 5

4 cooking apples, peeled, cored and thinly sliced
100 g/4 oz mincemeat
100 g/4 oz fresh brown breadcrumbs
100 g/4 oz soft brown sugar
1 teaspoon ground cinnamon
2 teaspoons grated orange rind
50 g/2 oz butter, cut into pieces
2 tablespoons cider
TO DECORATE:
4 small macaroons
icing sugar

1. Place a layer of half the apple slices on the bottom of a casserole and spread over half the mincemeat.
2. Mix together the breadcrumbs, sugar, cinnamon and orange rind and sprinkle half over the mincemeat. Scatter with half the butter.
3. Repeat the layers, ending with butter. Pour in the cider. Cover the casserole and cook in a preheated oven for 45 minutes.
4. Remove the lid and continue cooking for 15 minutes to colour the top.
5. Serve decorated with the macaroons, dusted with icing sugar.

SUSSEX PUDDLE PUDDING

Preparation time: 10 minutes
Cooking time: 1¾ hours
Oven: 160°C, 325°F, Gas Mark 3

225 g/8 oz self-raising flour, sifted
100 g/4 oz shredded suet
pinch of salt
25 g/1 oz granulated sugar
1 lemon, washed, cut into 8 pieces
100 g/4 oz soft brown sugar
100 g/4 oz butter, cut into pieces
1 tablespoon sifted icing sugar

1. Mix together the flour, suet, salt and granulated sugar and mix to a soft dough with water. Turn on to a floured surface.
2. Cut off two-thirds of the dough and roll out to line a 1.2 litre/2 pint casserole dish. Layer the lemon pieces into the dish with the soft brown sugar and butter.
3. Roll out the remaining dough and cover the filling.
4. Butter a piece of foil, pleat it and tie over the casserole. Place the casserole in a roasting tin half filled with hot water and cook in a preheated oven for 1¾ hours.
5. Remove the foil and dust the pudding with icing sugar. Serve from the casserole, with custard or cream.

CHOCOLATE ALMOND PUDDING

P

Preparation time: 20 minutes
Cooking time: steaming 15 minutes
L pressure 30 minutes

100 g/4 oz caster sugar
100 g/4 oz margarine
2 eggs, beaten
½ teaspoon almond essence
100 g/4 oz self-raising flour
2 tablespoons cocoa powder
25 g/1 oz blanched almonds
900 ml/1½ pints boiling water
little lemon juice or vinegar
SAUCE:
100 g/4 oz plain chocolate, broken into small pieces
knob of butter
3 tablespoons milk
2 tablespoons golden syrup
1 teaspoon vanilla essence

1. Cream the sugar and margarine together until light and fluffy. Beat in the eggs a little at a time with the almond essence.
2. Sift the flour with the cocoa powder and fold into the creamed mixture.
3. Reserve six of the almonds and chop the remainder. Fold the chopped almonds into the mixture.
4. Lightly grease a 900 ml/1½ pint pudding basin. Arrange the reserved whole almonds in a pattern over the bottom. Add the pudding mixture and smooth the top.
5. Cover with a double layer of greased greaseproof paper or a piece of greased foil and tie on securely.
6. Put the trivet in the cooker, rim side down, and pour in the water and lemon juice or vinegar. Bring to the boil, then place the pudding on the trivet.

7. Close the cooker and steam for 15 minutes (without the weight). Raise the heat, bring to L pressure and cook for 30 minutes. Reduce the pressure slowly.
8. To make the sauce, put all the ingredients in a small saucepan. Heat gently, stirring, until the chocolate has melted and the sauce is smooth.
9. Turn the pudding on to a heated serving dish and serve with the sauce.

Above left: Brown Betty
Above right: Sussex puddle pudding

Right: Chocolate almond pudding

ORANGE SPONGE PUDDING

P

Preparation time: 20 minutes
Cooking time: steaming 15 minutes
* L pressure 30 minutes*

100 g/4 oz butter or margarine
100 g/4 oz caster sugar
2 eggs, beaten
150 g/6 oz self-raising flour,
  sifted
finely grated rind and juice of
  1 orange
2 tablespoons orange
  marmalade
900 ml/1½ pints boiling water
little lemon juice or vinegar

1. Cream the butter or margarine and sugar together until light and fluffy. Beat in the eggs a little at a time.
2. Fold in the flour with the orange rind and, lastly, the orange juice.
3. Lightly grease a 900 ml/1½ pint pudding basin. Put the marmalade in the bottom and cover with the sponge mixture.
4. Cover the pudding with a double layer of greased greaseproof paper or a piece of greased foil. Tie on securely.

5. Put the trivet in the cooker, rim side down, and pour in the water and lemon juice or vinegar. Bring to the boil, then place the pudding on the trivet and close the cooker.
6. Steam the pudding for 15 minutes (without the weight). Raise the heat, bring to L pressure and cook for 30 minutes. Reduce the pressure slowly.
7. Turn out the pudding on to a heated serving dish. Serve with hot custard.

Right: Orange sponge pudding

QUEEN OF PUDDINGS

Preparation time: 20 minutes
Cooking time: 50 minutes
Oven: 180℃, 350°F, Gas Mark 4

450 ml/¾ pint milk
50 g/2 oz butter
225 g/8 oz caster sugar
90 g/3½ oz fresh breadcrumbs
  or cake crumbs
grated rind of ½ lemon
3 eggs, separated
2 tablespoons strawberry jam

1. In a small saucepan, heat together the milk, butter and 50 g/2 oz of the sugar, stirring to dissolve the sugar. Pour the mixture on to the crumbs.
2. Add the lemon rind and egg yolks and mix well together. Pour into a 20 cm/8 inch casserole, cover and cook in a preheated oven for 35 minutes or until set.
3. Leave to cool slightly, then spread with the jam.

4. Whisk the egg whites until stiff. Add 75 g/3 oz of the remaining sugar and whisk again until very stiff. Fold in the rest of the sugar. Spread the meringue over the jam.
5. Return the casserole, uncovered, to the oven and cook for a further 15 minutes to colour the meringues. Serve from the casserole.

PLUM MERINGUE PIE

Preparation time: 20 minutes
Cooking time: 1¼ hours
Oven: 180℃, 350°F, Gas Mark 4;
* reduced to 140℃, 275°F, Gas*
* Mark 1*

450 g/1 lb cooking plums,
  stoned and halved
grated rind and juice of 1 orange
225 g/8 oz caster sugar
2 tablespoons red wine
100 g/4 oz fresh breadcrumbs or
  plain cake crumbs
2 eggs, separated
50 g/2 oz butter, softened
vanilla essence
TO DECORATE:
glacé cherries (optional)
crystallized angelica (optional)

1. Put the plums, orange rind and juice, 100 g/4 oz of the sugar and the red wine into a 20 cm/8 inch casserole. Cover and cook in a preheated oven for 30 minutes.
2. Drain the fruit, reserving the juice. Place the crumbs in a bowl, add the fruit juice, egg yolks and butter and beat well together. Mix in the fruit. Pour back into the casserole.
3. Whisk the egg whites until stiff. Add 50 g/2 oz of the remaining sugar and a few drops of vanilla essence and beat again until very stiff. Fold in the remaining sugar.
4. Spread the meringue over the fruit mixture in the casserole and dust with a little extra sugar. Lower the oven temperature and bake the pie for 45 minutes or until crisp.
5. Decorate with glacé cherries and angelica, if using.

Right: Queen of puddings
Far right: Plum meringue pie

TUTTI FRUTTI BREAD PUDDING P

Preparation time: 20 minutes
Cooking time: H pressure 5 minutes

8 thick slices of white bread, crusts removed
50 g/2 oz butter or soft (tub) margarine
1 × 215 g/7½ oz can sliced peaches, drained
25 g/1 oz glacé cherries, chopped
50 g/2 oz seedless raisins
½ teaspoon ground cinnamon
2 eggs (size 2)
300 ml/½ pint milk
2 tablespoons caster sugar
300 ml/½ pint boiling water
little lemon juice or vinegar

1. Spread the slices of bread with the butter or margarine. Cut each slice into quarters.
2. Lightly grease a straight-sided 1.2 litre/2 pint ovenproof soufflé dish (or suitable size container to fit the cooker).
3. Put half the bread into the dish. Cover with a layer of half the fruits and sprinkle over half of the cinnamon. Repeat the layers, making a pattern with the peach slices on the top.
4. Beat together the eggs, milk and 1 tablespoon of the sugar. Pour over the bread and fruit and leave to stand for 5 minutes.
5. Cover with a piece of greased greaseproof paper or foil and tie on securely.
6. Put the trivet into the cooker, rim side down, and pour in the water and lemon juice or vinegar. Bring to the boil, then place the pudding on the trivet.
7. Close the cooker, bring to H pressure and cook for 5 minutes. Reduce the pressure slowly.
8. Lift out the pudding and remove the covering. Sprinkle the top with the remaining sugar and brown lightly under a hot grill.
9. Serve hot or cold, with whipped cream.

Top left: Tutti frutti bread pudding
Top right: Pineapple crush puddings
Right: Wholemeal spiced roll

WHOLEMEAL SPICED ROLL P

Preparation time: 15 minutes
Cooking time: steaming 10 minutes
* L pressure 25 minutes*

100 g/4 oz wholemeal flour
50 g/2 oz fresh white breadcrumbs
75 g/3 oz shredded suet
2 teaspoons baking powder
1 teaspoon ground mixed spice
1 tablespoon caster sugar
about 4 tablespoons milk
50 g/2 oz sultanas
25 g/1 oz currants
grated rind of 1 orange
900 ml/1½ pints boiling water
little lemon juice or vinegar

1. Mix together the flour, breadcrumbs, suet, baking powder, spice and sugar. Add enough of the milk to form a smooth dough that leaves the sides of the bowl clean.
2. Turn out the dough on to a floured board and knead lightly. Roll out into an oblong a little narrower than the bottom of the cooker and about 1 cm/½ inch thick.
3. Spread the dried fruit and orange rind over the dough. Dampen the edges with milk and roll up like a Swiss roll, sealing the edges well.
4. Place, seam side down, on a well-greased piece of foil or double thickness of greased greaseproof paper.

Wrap loosely, making a pleat in the centre to allow for expansion, and seal the ends well.
5. Place the trivet in the cooker, rim side down, and pour in the water and lemon juice or vinegar. Bring to the boil, then place the pudding on the trivet.
6. Close the cooker and steam for 10 minutes (without the weight). Raise the heat, bring to L pressure and cook for 25 minutes. Reduce the pressure slowly.
7. Turn out the roll on to a heated serving dish. Serve with butter and brown sugar.

PINEAPPLE CRUSH PUDDINGS $\boxed{\text{S}}$

Serves: 4-6
Preparation time: 20 minutes
Cooking time: High 3-4 hours

100 g/4 oz butter or margarine
100 g/4 oz caster sugar
2 eggs, beaten
150 g/6 oz self-raising flour, sifted
1 × 225 g/8 oz can crushed pineapple
450 ml/¾ pint boiling water
5 tablespoons cold water
2 teaspoons cornflour

1. Preheat the stoneware pot for about 15 minutes while preparing the ingredients.
2. Cream the butter or margarine and sugar together until light and fluffy.
3. Beat in the eggs a little at a time, then fold in the flour.
4. Lightly grease 6 small or 4 medium teacups. Drain the pineapple well, reserving the juice. Put 2 teaspoons of pineapple in the bottom of each cup.
5. Divide the creamed mixture between the cups, filling them no more than two-thirds full.
6. Cover each pudding with a double thickness of greased greaseproof paper or a piece of greased foil. Tie on securely.

7. Put the puddings in the stoneware pot. Pour boiling water around them.
8. Cover and cook on High for 3-4 hours.
9. To make the sauce, put the remaining pineapple and the reserved juice into a small saucepan with 4 tablespoons of the water. Dissolve the cornflour in the remaining water and stir into the pineapple. Bring to the boil, stirring, and simmer for 1 minute or until thickened.
10. Turn out the cooked puddings on to a heated serving dish. Pour the hot sauce over them and serve.

HOT SUMMER PUDDING

Preparation time: 20 minutes
plus overnight pressing
Cooking time: 1½ hours
Oven: 180°C, 350°F, Gas Mark 4

1 kg/2 lb blackcurrants,
 fresh or frozen
225 g/8 oz sugar
grated rind of ½ lemon
8 trifle sponge cakes, sliced

1. Put the blackcurrants, sugar and lemon rind into a straight-sided 20 cm/8 inch casserole. Cover and cook in a preheated oven for 30 minutes.
2. Pour the fruit into a bowl.
3. Wash the casserole and rinse in cold water; do not dry. Line the bottom and sides of the casserole with most of the sponge cake slices. Pour in the fruit. Cover the top with the remaining cake slices.
4. Put a piece of foil over the top, then a weight. Leave overnight.
5. Remove the weight and foil. Cover with the casserole lid and cook in a preheated oven for 45 minutes. Serve from the dish with double cream.

STUFFED PEAR CONDÉ

Preparation time: 15 minutes
Cooking time: 2 hours 20 minutes
Oven: 160°C, 325°F, Gas Mark 3

50 g/2 oz short grain rice
600 ml/1 pint milk
50 g/2 oz sugar
few drops of almond essence
50 g/2 oz ground almonds
1 tablespoon clear honey
1 × 425 g/15 oz can pears,
 drained and juice reserved
1 tablespoon apricot jam
2 teaspoons cornflour
25 g/1 oz flaked almonds

1. Put the rice, milk, sugar and almond essence in a casserole and stir well. Cover and cook in a preheated oven for 2 hours or until the rice is tender.
2. Mix together the ground almonds and enough honey to make a stiff paste. Fill the hollows of the pears and place on the rice.
3. Mix 4 tablespoons of the pear juice with the apricot jam in a saucepan.
4. Dissolve the cornflour in a little more of the pear juice and add to the pan. Bring to the boil, stirring, then pour over the stuffed pears. Sprinkle with the almonds.
5. Return the casserole, uncovered, to the oven and cook for 15-20 minutes or until the almonds are golden.

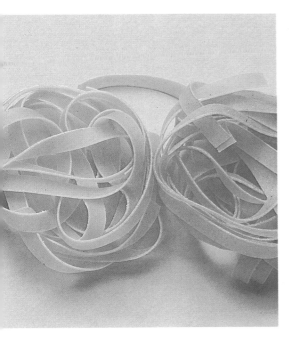

FRUIT NOODLE

Preparation time: 30 minutes
Cooking time: 30 minutes
Oven: 180°C, 350°F, Gas Mark 4

225 g/8 oz ribbon noodles
  (fettucine)
100 g/4 oz sugar
50 g/2 oz seedless raisins
½ teaspoon ground cinnamon
pinch of ground ginger
50 g/2 oz walnuts, chopped
50 g/2 oz butter, softened
2 eggs, beaten
1 × 425 g/15 oz can pineapple
  slices, drained and juice
  reserved
1 teaspoon arrowroot
1 tablespoon Kirsch (optional)

1. Cook the noodles in boiling water until tender. Drain well, then tip into a large bowl.
2. Add the sugar, raisins, spices, walnuts, butter and eggs and mix well.
3. Put the pineapple slices on the bottom of a greased casserole. Top with the noodle mixture. Cover and cook in a preheated oven for 20 minutes.
4. Remove the lid and cook for a further 10 minutes to colour the top.
5. Meanwhile, dissolve the arrowroot in a little of the pineapple juice and pour the remaining juice into a saucepan.
6. Bring to the boil, then stir in the arrowroot and simmer until thick.
7. Remove from the heat and stir in the Kirsch, if using. Serve this sauce with the pudding.

PERSIAN RICE PUDDING

Preparation time: 15 minutes
Cooking time: about 2 hours
Oven: 160°C, 325°F, Gas Mark 3

600 ml/1 pint milk
4 tablespoons short grain rice
2 tablespoons caster sugar
1 vanilla pod, or
½ teaspoon vanilla essence
1 teaspoon ground coriander
25 g/1 oz pistachio nuts,
 skinned and chopped
150 ml/¼ pint double cream,
 lightly whipped
1 tablespoon sweet sherry
crystallized violets, to decorate
 (optional)

1. Put the milk, rice, sugar and vanilla into a casserole and stir well.
2. Cover and cook in a preheated oven for 2 hours or until the rice is tender and almost all the milk has been absorbed.
3. Pour the rice mixture into a bowl and leave until cold. Remove the vanilla pod, if used.
4. Beat the coriander into the rice. Stir in the pistachios, cream and sherry. Transfer to a glass dish and chill well.
5. Decorate with crystallized violets.

CHOCOLATE CUPS $\boxed{S}$

Preparation time: 15 minutes
Cooking time: Low 4-5 hours

300 ml/½ pint milk
150 ml/¼ pint single cream
75 g/3 oz plain chocolate,
    broken into small pieces
3 eggs (size 2), beaten
25 g/1 oz caster sugar
1 teaspoon vanilla essence
300 ml/½ pint boiling water
TO DECORATE:
150 ml/¼ pint double cream,
    whipped until stiff
1 tablespoon coarsely grated
    plain chocolate

1. Preheat the stoneware pot for about 15 minutes while preparing the ingredients.
2. Put the milk, cream and chocolate into a heavy-based saucepan. Heat until almost boiling, then remove from the heat and stir until the chocolate has melted.
3. Beat together the eggs, sugar and vanilla essence. Add the hot milk mixture and mix thoroughly.
4. Lightly grease 4 teacups. Strain the custard into the cups and cover each cup with a piece of foil.
5. Stand the cups in the stoneware pot and pour the boiling water around them.
6. Cover and cook on Low for 4-5 hours.
7. Lift out the cups, remove the foil and chill thoroughly.
8. Turn out the custards and decorate with the whipped cream and grated chocolate.

BAKED BANANA TRIFLE $\boxed{S}$

Preparation time: 15 minutes
Cooking time: Low 3-4 hours

1 jam Swiss roll, cut into 12
    slices
2 tablespoons medium sherry
3 bananas, peeled and sliced
3 eggs
300 ml/½ pint milk
1 tablespoon caster sugar
½ teaspoon vanilla essence
300 ml/½ pint boiling water
25 g/1 oz flaked almonds,
    toasted

1. Preheat the stoneware pot for about 15 minutes while preparing the ingredients.
2. Lightly grease a 1.2 litre/2 pint dish (a soufflé dish is ideal).
3. Cover the bottom of the dish with half the Swiss roll slices and sprinkle with 1 tablespoon of the sherry.
4. Cover the Swiss roll with the sliced bananas, then add another layer of Swiss roll slices and sprinkle with the remaining sherry.
5. Beat together the eggs, milk, sugar and vanilla essence. Pour evenly over the ingredients in the dish.
6. Cover with a double layer of greased greaseproof paper or a piece of greased foil. Tie on securely.
7. Pour the boiling water into the stoneware pot. Add the pudding.
8. Cover and cook on Low for 3-4 hours (4 hours is the maximum time for best results).
9. Lift out the dish, remove the covering and chill the trifle thoroughly. Serve sprinkled with the toasted almonds.

Below left: Persian rice pudding
Below right: Chocolate cups
Bottom: Baked banana trifle

SUMMER COMPÔTE S

Serves: 4-6
Preparation time: 15 minutes
Cooking time: Low 4-5 hours
  High 2-2½ hours

450 g/1 lb rhubarb,
  cut into 2.5 cm/1 inch pieces
225 g/8 oz gooseberries,
  topped and tailed
100 g/4 oz cherries
2 dessert apples, peeled, cored
  and cut into eighths
finely grated rind of 1 orange
2 tablespoons orange juice
2 tablespoons sugar
150 ml/¼ pint water

1. Put all the fruit into the stoneware pot and add the remaining ingredients. Stir well.
2. Cover and cook on Low for 4-5 hours or High for 2-2½ hours.
3. Serve hot with custard, or well chilled with whipped cream.

Right: Summer compôte
Far right: Apricot and almond dessert

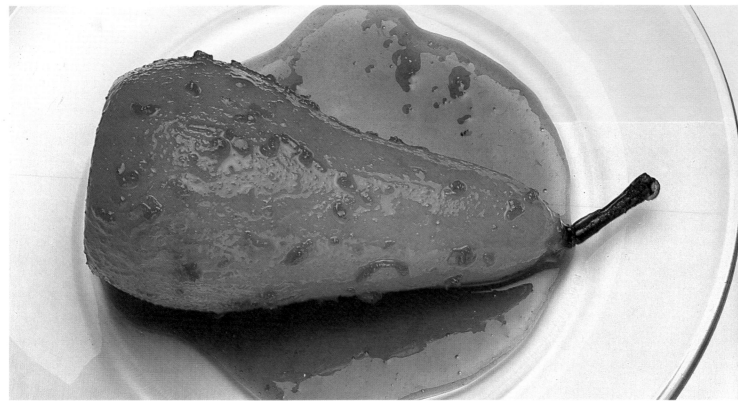

PEARS IN PORT P

Preparation time: 10 minutes,
  plus chilling time
Cooking time: H pressure 6 minutes

4 dessert pears, with stalks
finely grated rind and juice of
  2 lemons
6 tablespoons port
6 tablespoons water
2 tablespoons sugar

If using cooking pears for this recipe allow 8 minutes at H pressure.

1. Carefully peel the pears, leaving the stalks intact.
2. Put the lemon rind and juice, port, water and sugar into the cooker and stir thoroughly. Stand the pears in the cooker and spoon the liquid over them.
3. Close the cooker, bring to H pressure and cook for 6 minutes. Reduce the

pressure quickly.
4. Carefully lift out the pears and stand them in a serving dish.
5. Return the open cooker to the heat and boil the liquid rapidly for 2-3 minutes or until it becomes syrupy. Pour over the pears and chill.
6. Serve with whipped cream.

APRICOT & ALMOND DESSERT [S]

Serves: 6
Preparation time: 8 minutes,
  plus soaking time
Cooking time: Low 5-6 hours
  High 2½-3 hours

450 g/1 lb dried apricots
finely grated rind and juice of
  2 oranges
50 g/2 oz blanched almonds
2 tablespoons demerara sugar
300 ml/½ pint water
2 tablespoon brandy (optional)

1. Put the apricots into a bowl. Cover with boiling water and leave to soak for 1 hour. Drain.
2. Put the apricots into the stoneware pot and add the remaining ingredients. Stir well.
3. Cover and cook on Low for 5-6 hours or High for 2½-3 hours.
4. Serve hot or cold with whipped cream.

Above left: Pears in port
Above right: Figs in coffee

FIGS IN COFFEE [S]

Preparation time: 5 minutes,
  plus soaking time
Cooking time: Low 5-6 hours
  High 2½-3 hours

450 g/1 lb dried figs
boiling water
2 tablespoons instant coffee
  powder
450 ml/¾ pint boiling water
2 tablespoons demerara sugar

1. Put the figs into a bowl. Pour over enough boiling water to cover and leave to soak for 1 hour. Drain and discard the liquid.
2. Put the figs into the stoneware pot. Mix together the instant coffee, boiling water and sugar and pour over the figs.
3. Cover and cook on Low for 5-6 hours or High for 2½-3 hours.
4. Pour the figs into a dish and chill well before serving.

TOPPINGS & ACCOMPANIMENTS

SEASONED CRUMBS

Preparation time: 10 minutes
Cooking time: 8 minutes

50 g/2 oz butter
1 small onion,
    peeled and finely chopped
225 g/8 oz fresh brown
    breadcrumbs
50 g/2 oz Parmesan cheese,
    grated
1 teaspoon dry mustard
salt
freshly ground black pepper

Use as a topping for recipes such as Smoked Mackerel Ramekins (page 45), Vegetarian Casserole (page 79) and Aubergine Layer (page 104).

1. Melt the butter in a frying pan, add the onion and cook until softened.
2. Stir in the remaining ingredients and season to taste with salt and pepper. Cool.
3. Store in a covered jar in the refrigerator for up to 1 month. Freeze up to 3 months.

CHEESE STRAW PASTRY

Preparation time: 10 minutes

175 g/6 oz plain flour, sifted
salt
freshly ground black pepper
pinch of cayenne
100 g/4 oz butter, cut into pieces
25 g/1 oz Parmesan cheese,
    grated
25 g/1 oz Cheddar cheese,
    grated
1 egg yolk

Use this pastry for Chicken with Artichoke (page 50).

1. Sift the flour into a bowl, and season with salt, pepper and cayenne. Rub in the butter until the mixture resembles breadcrumbs. Add the cheeses.
2. Mix to a firm dough with the egg yolk and a few drops of water, if necessary.
3. Roll out on a floured surface and cut into straws or lattice.

HOT GARLIC BREAD

Preparation time: 10 minutes
Cooking time: 20 minutes
Oven: 200°C, 400°F, Gas Mark 6

100 g/4 oz butter, softened
3 garlic cloves,
    peeled and crushed
salt
freshly ground black pepper
1 small stick French bread

1. Cream together the butter, garlic and a little salt and pepper.
2. Cut the loaf into 5 cm/2 inch slices to within 1 cm/½ inch of the bottom.
3. Spread the butter between the slices and over the top of the loaf, then wrap loosely in foil.
4. Bake in a preheated moderately hot oven for 15 minutes. Uncover the top of the loaf and bake for a further 5 minutes to crisp.
5. Serve hot with Fish Stew Provençale (page 42) or use any of these breads to complement a casserole which is being served with a salad.

VARIATIONS:

ANCHOVY LOAF
Substitute 1 × 25 g/1 oz tube of anchovy paste for the garlic and omit the salt and pepper.

HERB LOAF
Substitute 2 tablespoons chopped fresh herbs for the garlic.

HERB & NUT DUMPLINGS

Preparation time: 10 minutes

50 g/2 oz self-raising flour, sifted
50 g/2 oz fresh white breadcrumbs
50 g/2 oz shredded suet
25 g/1 oz walnuts, or other nuts, chopped
1 tablespoon chopped fresh herbs
salt
freshly ground black pepper
1 egg (sizes 5, 6), beaten

These go particularly well with lamb dishes and should be added to the casserole for the final 30-40 minutes.

1. Mix together the flour, breadcrumbs, suet, walnuts and herbs and season to taste with salt and pepper.
2. Mix to a soft dough with the egg, then form into small balls.

COTTAGE CHEESE DUMPLINGS

Preparation time: 10 minutes

100 g/4 oz cottage cheese, sieved
25 g/1 oz butter, melted
2 teaspoons paprika
1 teaspoon caraway seeds
salt
freshly ground black pepper
75 g/3 oz plain flour, sifted
1 egg (sizes 5, 6), beaten

These are particularly good with beef dishes and should be added to the casserole for the final 30-40 minutes.

1. Beat together the cheese and butter. Add the paprika and caraway seeds and season to taste with salt and pepper.
2. Stir in the flour and mix with enough beaten egg to form a soft dough. Form into small balls.

SAUSAGE MEATBALLS

Preparation time: 10 minutes
Cooking time: about 10 minutes

175 g/3 oz sausage meat
½ teaspoon chopped fresh sage
salt
freshly ground black pepper
1 egg (sizes 5, 6), beaten
25 g/1 oz seasoned flour
2 tablespoons oil

Use as an accompaniment to recipes such as Sauerkraut and Pork Goulash (page 87).

1. Mix the sausage meat with the sage and a little salt and pepper. Bind with the beaten egg. Form into small balls and roll in the seasoned flour.
2. Heat the oil in a large frying pan, add the meat balls and brown on all sides.
3. Freeze up to 3 months.

FRIED CROÛTONS

Preparation time: 5 minutes
Cooking time: 5 minutes

4 tablespoons oil
4 thick slices bread, crusts removed, cut into 1 cm/½ inch dice

Use fried croûtons and the herb and garlic variations to garnish casseroles such as Quick Chicken Hash (page 41), Kidney and Sausage Braise (page 33), Coq au Vin (page 49), Casserole of Scallops with Cream (page 66) and Prawn Gumbo with Rice (page 117). The cheese croûtons go well with a dish such as Beef with Guinness (page 12).

1. Heat the oil in a large frying pan, add the diced bread and toss over a brisk heat until crisp and golden.
2. Drain on kitchen paper.

VARIATIONS:

HERB CROUTONS
Toss the cooked croûtons in a chopped fresh herb of your choice.

GARLIC CROUTONS
Add 1 garlic clove, peeled and crushed, to the oil for cooking.

CHEESE CROUTONS
Toss the cooked croûtons in finely grated cheese.

INDEX

A

American beef and cheese
  casserole 12
Anchovy loaf 140
Apple:
  Brown betty 128
  Chicken Normandy 125
  Normandy apple pudding 89
  Old-fashioned apple pudding
    126
  Pork chops Bramley-style 22
  Pork Pippin 54
Apricot:
  Apricot and almond dessert 139
  Apricot stuffed pork chops 55
  Pigeons with apricots 46
Artichokes, chicken with 50
Aubergine layer 104

B

Bacon:
  Bacon and butter bean casserole
    23
  Bacon pot roast 34
  Bacon and sausage special 26
  Irish hot pot 23
  Savoury bacon and onion roll 27
  Smoky chicken parcels 40
  Theatre supper 24
Bamia and lamb casserole 94
Banana:
  Baked banana trifle 137
Barbecue chicken with saffron rice
  78
Bean:
  Bacon and butter bean casserole
    23
  Butter beans Breton 102
  Cassoulet 18
  Continental bean salad 114
  Fabada 91
  Green beans provençale 110
  Mixed bean casserole 102
  Pork and bean hot pot 75
  Spare ribs with beans 20
  Sweet sour pork and bean bake
    118
Beef:
  American beef and cheese
    casserole 12
  Beef Dubonnet 14
  Beef with Guinness 12
  Beef and horseradish cream
    casserole 12
  Beef Java 13
  Beef with Madeira and
    mushroom sauce 59
  Beef marinated in wine 59
  Beef and pepper casserole 15
  Beef, sage and ham roulades 61
  Braised beef with orange 14
  Chinese spiced beef 119
  Country beef and herby bread 70
  Gingered beef patties 61
  Hungarian meatball and potato
    casserole 71
  Italian beef casserole 121
  Mexican meatballs 121

Minced beef Napoli 70
Moulded spiced beef 60
New England beef dinner 68
Pot au feu 39
Rich beef and kidney casserole
  13
Roman pie 120
Russian cabbage 10
Spiced braised beef with
  vegetables 71
Beetroot, scalloped 111
Brown Betty 128
Brunswick stew 76
Butter beans Breton 102

C

Cabbage:
  Casserole of red cabbage with
    Austrian sausage 122
  Ham and cabbage casserole 25
  Mock dolmas 99
  Portuguese cabbage and potato
    soup 90
  Russian cabbage 10
  Spiced cabbage 106
Carrot and walnut bake 107
Cassoulet 18
Cataplana 91
Celery, braised 99
Cheese croûtons 141
Cheese dumplings 101
Cheese straw pastry 140
Cherry:
  Braised venison with Morello
    cherries 58
  Jubilee duckling 56
Chestnuts, apples and prunes,
  casserole of 106
Chick pea casserole, Mexican 95
Chicken:
  Barbecue chicken with saffron
    rice 78
  Chicken with artichokes 50
  Chicken casserole 41
  Chicken in cider cream sauce 52
  Chicken korma 85
  Chicken marengo 50
  Chicken Normandy 125
  Coq au vin 49
  Curried drumsticks 124
  Hungarian chicken 86
  Malayan chicken 84
  Poached chicken with sauce
    supreme 51
  Poulet citron 51
  Quick chicken hash 41
  Smoky chicken parcels 40
  Stuffed chicken 38
  Stuffed chicken drumsticks 38
Chinese lamb 82
Chinese pork ribs 118
Chinese spiced beef 119
Chocolate almond pudding 128
Chocolate cups 137
Cod:
  Cod alla romana 92
  Cod and potato bake 80
  Curried fish ring 116
  New England chowder 95

Continental bean salad 114
Coq au vin 49
Cottage cheese dumplings 141
Country beef and herby bread 70
Country casserole 26
Croûtons, fried 141
Crumbs, seasoned 140
Curried dishes:
  Curried drumsticks 124
  Curried fish ring 116
  Curried fruit casserole 100
  Mixed vegetable curry 100

D

Devilled veal 76
Duckling:
  Duckling with oranges 56
  Jubilee duckling 56
Dumplings:
  Cheese dumplings 101
  Cottage cheese dumplings 141
  Herb and nut dumplings 141
  Sage dumplings 75

E

Electric slow cookers 7-8

F

Fabada 91
Fennel, braised veal with 65
Figs in coffee 139
Fish. See also Cod, etc.
  Curried fish ring 116
  Fish casserole 81
  Fish stew provençale 42
  Hot fish dip 116
  Mixed fish casserole with
    mustard cream 42
Frankfurters Vichy 25
Frikadeller 87
Fruit. See also Apple, Apricot, etc.
  Curried fruit casserole 100
  Fruit noodle 135
  Rum fruit punch 125
  Summer compôte 138

G

Gammon:
  Autumn ham 122
  Gingered gammon 112
  Orange and port wine gammon
    53
Garlic bread, hot 140
Garlic croûtons 141
Gingered beef patties 61
Ginered gammon 112
Greek-style peppers 105
Green beans provençale 110

H

Haddock:
  Smoked haddock special 45
Ham. See also Gammon
  Autumn ham 122
  Beef, sage and ham roulades 61
  Ham and cabbage casserole 25
  Ham and potato St Germain 109
  Hawaiian ham 24
  Theatre supper 24
Hare:
  Casserole of hare 57
Hasenpfeffer 30
Hawaiian ham 24
Heart:
  Lemon hearts 37
  Mock goose 37
Herb croûtons 141
Herb loaf 140
Herb and nut dumplings 141
Hungarian chicken 86
Hungarian meatball and potato
  casserole 71

I

Irish hot pot 23
Italian beef casserole 121
Italian vegetables 104

J

Jambalaya 94
Jubilee duckling 56

K

Kasha, pork and tomato with 21
Kidney:
  Kidney and sausage braise 33
  Kidney and vegetable hot pot 34
  Kidneys Napoleon 62
  Lamb's kidney and mushroom
    braise 36
  Rich beef and kidney casserole
    13

L

Lamb:
  Bamia and lamb casserole 94
  Breast of lamb ragoût 17
  Cassoulet 18
  Chinese lamb 82
  Lamb casserole 72
  Lamb, leek and potato casserole
    72
  Lamb and lemon casserole 62
  Lamb romana 63
  Lancashire hot pot 16
  Moroccan lamb 123
  Scotch broth 73
  Spicy lamb 18

Tajine of lamb 63
Tomato lamb with cheese
    scalloped potatoes 73
Turkish pilaff 86
Winter lamb casserole 16
Lancashire hot pot 16
Leek:
    Lamb, leek and potato casserole
    72
    Rabbit and leeks 31
Lemon:
    Lamb and lemon casserole 62
    Lemon hearts 37
    Lemon pork 52
    Poulet citron 51
Lettuce:
    Braised luttuce 96
Liver:
    Continental liver casserole 32
    Lamb's liver with coriander 33
    Paprika liver casserole 34
    Scandinanvian liver 32

M

Mackerel:
    Orange mackerel bake 45
    Smoked mackerel ramekins 45
Malayan chicken 84
Marrow Madras 101
Meat. *See also* Beef, Lamb, etc.
    Fabada 91
    Pot au feu 39
    Puchero 77
Mexican chick pea casserole 95
Mexican meatballs 121
Mock dolmas 99
Mock goose 37
Moroccan lamb 123
Moulded spiced beef 60
Mulled wine 125
Mushroom:
    Lamb's kidney and mushroom
      braise 36
    Mushrooms à la grecque 115
Mussel:
    Moules marinière 66

N

Nasi goreng 85
New England beef dinner 68
New England chowder 95
Normandy apple pudding 89

O

Old-fashioned apple pudding 126
Onion:
    Onion sauce 26
    Savoury bacon and onion roll 27
    Stuffed Spanish onions 98
Orange:
    Braised beef with orange 14
    Duckling with oranges 56
    Orange mackerel bake 45
    Orange and port wine gammon
      53
    Orange sponge pudding 130
Osso bucco 28
Oxtail:
    Oxtail carbonnade 29
    Oxtail casserole 29
    Pot au feu 39

P

Paprika liver casserole 34
Paprika potatoes 110
Paupiettes de veau 88
Peach:
    Sicilian peaches 93
Pear:
    Pears in port 138
    Stuffed pear condé 134
Pepper:
    Beef and pepper casserole 15
    Greek-style peppers 105
    Pepper pork 19
Persian rice pudding 136
Pheasant in red wine 48
Pigeons with apricots 46
Pineapple crush puddings 133
Plaice mornay pie 80
Plum:
    Plum meringue pie 130
    Pork rashers with plums 22
Pork:
    Apricot stuffed pork chops 55
    Cassoulet 18
    Cataplana 91
    Chinese pork ribs 118
    Lemon pork 52
    Mexican chick pea casserole 95
    Nasi goreng 85
    Peppered pork 19
    Pork and bean hot pot 75
    Pork and brown rice pilau 74
    Pork casserole with sage
      dumplings 75
    Pork chops ardennaise 88
    Pork chops Bramley-style 22
    Pork with herb cream sauce 54
    Pork Pippin 54
    Pork rashers with plums 22
    Pork and tomato with kasha 21
    Pork and tomato pot roast 20
    Sauerkraut and pork goulash 87
    Spare ribs with beans 20
    Sweets sour pork and bean bake
      118
Potato:
    Cod and potato bake 80
    Ham and potato St Germain 109
    Hungarian meatball and potato
      casserole 71
    Paprika potatoes 110
    Pommes savoyarde 109
    Tomato lamb with cheese
      scalloped potatoes 73
Portuguese cabbage and potato
    soup 90
Pot au feu 39
Poulet citron 51
Poussins in sherry 49
Prawn:
    Prawn gumbo with rice 117
    Sole and prawn paupiettes 67
Pressure cookers 8-9
Puchero 77
Puddings:
    Apricot and almond dessert 139
    Baked banana trifle 137
    Brown Betty 128
    Chocolate almond pudding 128
    Chocolate cups 137
    Figs in coffee 139
    Fruit noodle 135
    Hot summer pudding 134
    Normandy apple pudding 89
    Old-fashioned apple pudding
      126

Orange sponge pudding 130
Pears in port 138
Persian rice pudding 136
Pineapple crush puddings 133
Plum meringue pie 130
Queen of puddings 130
Sicilian peaches 93
Stuffed pear condé 134
Summer compôte 138
Sussex puddle pudding 128
Tutti frutti bread pudding 132
Wholemeal spiced roll 132

Q

Queen of puddings 130

R

Rabbit:
    Brunswick stew 76
    Hasenpfeffer 30
    Rabbit and leeks 31
    Rabbit and tarragon fricassée 30
Red cabbage with Austrian
    sausage casserole 122
Rice:
    Persian rice pudding 136
    Pork and brown rice pilau 74
    Prawn gumbo with rice 117
    Risotto 103
    Saffron rice 78
    Sweetbreads with rice 78
    Tuna and corn risotto 81
    Turkish pilaff 86
Roman pie 120
Rum fruit punch 125
Russian cabbage 10

S

Saffron rice 78
Sage dumplings 75
Sauerkraut and pork goulash 87
Sausage:
    Bacon and sausage special 26
    Country casserole 26
    Frankfurters Vichy 25
    Kidney and sausage braise 33
    Sausage meatballs 141
Scallops:
    Casserole of scallops with cream
      66
Scalloped beetroot 111
Scandinavian liver 32
Scotch broth 73
Seafood casserole 43
Seafood chowder 117
Seasoned crumbs 140
Sicilian peaches 93
Smoked haddock special 45
Smoked mackerel ramekins 45
Smoky chicken parcels 40
Sole and prawn paupiettes 67
Soup:
    New England chowder 95
    Portuguese cabbage and potato
      soup 90
    Scotch broth 73
Spare ribs with beans 20

Spiced braised beef with
    vegetables 71
Spiced cabbage 106
Spicy lamb 18
Stuffed chicken 38
Stuffed chicken drumsticks 38
Stuffed pear condé 134
Stuffed Spanish onions 98
Summer compôte 138
Summer pudding, hot 134
Sussex puddle pudding 128
Sweet sour pork and bean bake 118
Sweetbreads:
    Sweetbreads au gratin 35
    Sweetbreads with rice 78

T

Tajine of lamb 63
Theatre supper 24
Tomato:
    Pork and tomato with kasha 21
    Pork and tomato pot roast 20
    Tomato and courgette casserole
      104
    Tomato lamb with cheese
      scalloped potatoes 73
Tongue with Madeira 60
Trout in white wine 67
Tuna:
    Tuna antipasto 92
    Tuna and corn risotto 81
Turkey:
    Turkey amandine 114
    Turkey Mexicana 40
    Turkey terrine 115
    Turkey Veronique 53
Turkish pilaff 86
Tutti frutti bread pudding 132

V

Veal:
    Braised veal with fennel 65
    Devilled veal 76
    Frikadeller 87
    Osso bucco 28
    Paupiettes de veau 88
    Veal tokany 65
    Veal in Vermouth 64
    Veau Veronique 64
Vegetable: *See also* Artichoke, etc.
    Italian vegetables 104
    Mixed vegetable curry 100
    Spiced braised beef with
      vegetables 71
    Vegetable casserole with cheese
      dumplings 101
    Vegetable chop suey 109
    Vegetable scallop 110
Vegetarian casserole 79
Venison:
    Braised venison with Morello
      cherries 58

W

Walnut:
    Aubergine layer 104
    Carrot and walnut bake 107
Wholemeal spiced roll 132
Winter lamb casserole 16